Dedica

who always showe

Where The Blacktop Ends

© 2010, John R. Mizell
email ; john1948@wheretheblacktopends.org
bigfish1236@msn.com

Where The Blacktop Ends

John R. Mizell

John R. Mizell
Steve Stout

3

Going back used to seem so possible.

For the life of me, I still can't figure out why life was so anxious to run me outta paradise three different times. Even then sometimes, in the middle of the jungle, unable to see my own hand in front of my face, that tantalizing possibility of home was the only loose thumbtack my mind could hang on.

That person was just GONE four years later though, an' I didn't even know who that was anymore or how to bring them back. Fours years later I didn't even remember anybody from my high school class there...nobody. Maybe it was getting shot in the head. Maybe it was watching a lot of people I cared about die in hard ways. That person was missed, sometimes mourned, but I guess there's only moving forward once you've seen an' done enough killing.

Lord knows I tried. Waiting around for six months. Hanging on the promises of my Uncles. Waiting for life after death to start.

I shouldn't even be alive to WRITE this. Some people say I had a gift, but if it WAS a gift then the DEVIL was in the details. The gift of survival carries the curse of being surrounded by people without it. They disappear an' carry off pieces of your soul.

I've waited a long time to tell my story. Between wounds, agent orange, an' a little judiciously repenting of hard living, my time's been shortened an' I'm lucky to be alive right now, much less in a year or two. I guess it's time now. Maybe when you see this you can answer the only question I still ask, why am I still alive?

My first memory?

Well...I was with Mama on the porch of the house where the blacktop ended. We called it that because...that's where it was. Civilization ended right there in front of our house where the state paved blacktop dropped off onto a dirt road. You could stand there with one foot in the country an' one headed toward the city. We lived like that too.

For some reason she was holding a dove in one of her hands. She held it up an' released it into the cool evening sun. It was so beautiful, gleaming in the last light. I reached out to it.

Then it exploded.

That's the God's honest truth.

I'm from a place near Mobile, Alabama where the main roads were dirt. The memory of summers there still pulls at me like a Norman Rockwell calendar picture of a boy an' his dog. It was a town that didn't even have a name, an' still doesn't far as I know. People would just say "Where the blacktop ends on route 5." Since the blacktop ends somewhere else now, I suppose people close enough to call it anything just call it "up the road".

My Father was a hard working man with a pretty stern countenance. I imagine I could almost count on both hands the number of times I saw him laugh out loud. I don't even have a picture that he smiles in. We could still tell he loved us anyway, even though there was a LOT of us to go 'round.

We had four acres around our house that we played in. It provided a fair amount of work too since weeds didn't sleep, an' everything you WANTED to grow seemed like it had to be pumped, poked, watered, an' HOED up outta the ground. With seven brothers an' sisters there was ALWAYS a hand when it was needed, an' sometimes when it WASN'T.

Daddy had a civilian position with the Air Force at the nearby base. Seemed like he was always traveling to Chicago or Detroit, an' other places, on business he wasn't allowed to talk about. Something to do with cameras. The cold war was ON then son, an' we were keeping an EYE on people. I guess daddy made the eyes. That's what I always thought anyway.

He was always doing something to the house as well that we'd help on. I definitely remember us digging a septic tank so I know we installed the indoor plumbing, anyway.

Between those pastimes an' eight kids he kept pretty busy and that made it a real treat to have him to ourselves when we could! Some of my best memories are the times I had alone with my Daddy. Especially since I was smallish for my age an' had a stutterin' lisp. Those were two apparently unforgivable sins to a fair number of my peers so I didn't have many friends as a boy. Cousins an' Uncles were my friends an' confidants growing up.

Most morning's when I was little, couldn't a been more than four, I'd be awake an' dressed before sunrise an' RUN down the path ta Grandma's house. They still had a wood stove for a long time (Grandpa being a bit of a Luddite), an' I was proud to light the fire every day for Grandma. She'd make breakfast then an' we'd talk 'bout the day or she'd tell me stories.

Grandpa would come stomping in an' give HIS two cents a lot too, but I'd try to be out playing on their acreage with my cousins, uncles, an' their neighbors by then. He wasn't necessarily cantankerous, but there's a LOT a little boy can do to irritate a Hellfire an' Brimstone Assemblies of God preaching man.

He'd built two brick churches with his own preaching an' money, an' kept fifty acres of farm to deal with. Just about anybodies first impression of Grandpa was a BUSY MAN with DECIDEDLY little time for NONSENSE! His favorite form of revival against any perceived evil's of youth, AN' his favorite form of surefire cure for nonsense, were one an' the same…a generous dose of RAZOR strap!

He was considered wise by the majority of people in our little place. Short of going to a judge, people

—

would come from miles around to have him settle disputes for them.

He'd always wished for a hellfire an' brimstone preacher outta one of his sons too, but he'd been disappointed in one way or another (possibly in no small part due to unreasonable expectations) in the spiritual aspirations of about ALL his boys.

My own father had been no exception, having married a woman who had a child outta wedlock an' NOT by my father (a couple of BIG no-no's to my Grandpa). I guess he'd have preferred a good old fashioned shotgun wedding to that.

They only talked when they had to an' my Grandpa made sure I knew he had a low opinion of my Daddy. Grandpa an' me didn't talk much when I was little 'cause of that I guess. I found out later that while Grandpa gave land to 'is other children for their houses, my Daddy had to PAY for his.

Irene was my older sister, the child that Grandpa had a problem with. I'm not sure why ANYTHING could or should be blamed on a BABY (don't get me started on abortion), but Grandpa managed to push Irene away her whole life. Mama didn't do such a bad job of that either come to think of it.

I'm supposing it was at least partially due to Grandpa's influence that Irene didn't even come to live with us until she was five years old. That was a shame too 'cause she could' a used a preachers influence. It turned out she had a real TALENT for finding what

—

8

you could only rightly say were "shortcuts" through the rules.

One of the things we did together as children to make a little spending money was collect pecans an' sell them by the bag to a local store. They'd weigh out the burlap bag-full's an' pay by the pound.

Every day we spent filling our bags there were always a lot of other kids around doing the same, black an' white. There was this one little black boy in particular that would sit an' watch all day without saying a WORD. Quietest an' stillest little boy I ever saw. Irene saw him an' got her angle.

She paid him fifty cents to get in her burlap sack an' let her cover him with pecans! He was perfect for the job an' was MORE than willing to use his greatest talent for what must' a seemed like a small fortune to him.

They weighed out that bag at the store an' even complimented her on all the hard work! I forget how much money she got, but I remember we ALL got the big eyes when they counted out those dollars into her hand.

I'm pretty sure they didn't ship that boy to Mobile for nationwide distribution. He was pretty quiet though, so it's hard to say.

Irene was forever coming up with creative ways to get an edge. We couldn't help but admire her for that. I could go on 'bout her adventures all day, but I guess that'll have to be another book.

—

Where Irene was what you'd have to call the prune pit of my Grandpa's eye, his youngest son Roy was definitely the APPLE. My Uncle Roy was so close to my age that we were more like cousins. We fished, an' played together with his best friend Ronald Smith an' Ronald's little brother Buddy.

In the summers the curse of school was lifted, an' we all had the free run of the woods an' gullies around our community an' we made the MOST of it. In the small gorges there were sweet vines you could cut an' drink from, an' then swing on them out over the cuts in the ground like you were FLYIN'. I'd bet real money we got a good twenty feet off the ground on a good swing.

You had to develop some real "vine sense" though cause sometimes one would come loose at a bad moment. Sherriff gravity taught some harsh lessons to a few' a my friends that way.

The woods around my Grandpa's fifty acres were our own cauldron of new civilizations.

We'd build huts an' forts, building up stores of pine cones for mutually assured bruising. No matter how much deterrent we managed to create, or how willing some were to sue for peace, diplomacy would ALWAYS break down an' a highly satisfying hail of pine cones was the ONLY answer.

We'd come home black, blue, scratched red, an' SMILIN' from more than one of those trips. Only the most dedicated warriors would join up early in the

---

10

season when the pine cones were hard 'n green.

Sometimes we'd collect lightning bugs in a jar an' sleep outside with the fading glow of their primeval hopes for a nightlight.

A lot of Grandpa's fading hopes for a preacher outta his sons were riding on ROY. Roy was also just about my best friend an' greatest protector too, getting in ta all KINDS of trouble beatin' up bigger kids when they'd pick on me. Grandpa blamed me every time he got in trouble for it, probably figuring the apple didn't fall far from the tree.

Roy was such a calm boy otherwise, I think that might' a been how he let off steam. He appeared to thoroughly enjoy beating on people when there was a good enough cause.

I can tell you from hard experience that a boy with a stuttering lisp in a small Southern town in the late 50's got pecked on by the other kids like a white chicken in a coop full of reds. I got to be a pretty fair hand with a haymaker before I turned seven outta sheer NECESSITY.

The grownups weren't much better. My first teachers in grade school would actually SLAP me when I didn't speak right because that was their "bonafide cure" for my "recalcitrance". Clearly, I just didn't want to speak properly as far as they were concerned. Speech therapy was a real high science when an' where I was a kid.

There wasn't much sympathy from anybody else in that God awful place either. A lot of the other kids would just laugh when the teachers would slap an' berate me for my speech.

There was one boy though that came up to me after I'd had a particularly bad day. He just said "Why do they do that to you?" I didn't know an' I'm sure that's what I said when I finally got it out. "Well that's just wrong", he finished after a thoughtful minute. I looked up then.

He wasn't much more to look at than me, but it was the first time anybody in that school had said a kind word to me. Turned out he lived less than a quarter mile away. Well we got to playing an' before you know it I had a best friend!

His name was Ricky Wallace.

We had a number of adventures that were pretty big stuff ta us but only a couple 'bout got us killed. Now fishing is not something you'd think would be particularly dangerous, but leave it to a couple' a six year olds to find a way.

Fishing was something I loved to do with my daddy, but any excuse or company was good enough for me. Ricky Wallace an' me would go whenever we could not to far from everybody's favorite swimming hole. It seemed like every time we went there though, some girl or another would come along bothering us with noisy questions to scare off fish, or some bigger boys would come push us off if they liked our shady spot better than theirs.

One day we were fishing at a particular spot an' some girl came along jabbering 'bout something. Absolutely couldn't take a hint to save her life! She was in the middle of something 'bout her dolls, when me an' Ricky 'bout jumped outta our skin as she let out a full on, blood curdling SCREECH right next to us!

She took off running, leaving us scratching our heads for a minute or two until Ricky noticed a SNAKE in the TREE we were sitting under! We watched that critter for a few minutes an' the worst thing he did was flick his tongue out a little.

Well you might imagine we got to looking 'round, an' we could see a few more doing 'bout the same thing, basking an' flicking their tongues. Seemed to us like they were just enjoying a day at the stream like we were so we left them all alone an' got back down to fishing.

Ricky an' me got to talking on the way home an' decided that this might be a pretty good thing! If those snakes hung out in the trees here it was for sure 'bout any girls, an' a lot of boys besides, wouldn't be too interested in our little fishing spot.

Well...we stewed on that for a day or so then spread the word 'bout the worlds most dangerous tree snakes! We got on with people 'bout how the place was just infested with those critters.

The little girl that'd been clever enough to discover the

—

terror from above turned out to be a willing an' talented accomplice. Once we started the story she ran with it like a dog that'd got off with a Christmas ham!

She went on like you wouldn't believe 'bout poisonous tree climbing monkey snakes that would drop right in your mouth if you looked up! She got herself a good audience with her initial efforts, so she plain old EXPANDED on it, painting up a scenes of reptile ARMAGEDDON with giant devil serpents flying outta the trees, hissing like gator's, an' spewing big old streams of deadly poison outta six inch fangs! We just nodded our heads an' agreed with everything she said.

Before you know it we had our own private fishing spot complete with flying, throat crawling, deadly poisonous monkey snake, security guards! We were considered brave souls for daring the gauntlet, an' the little fish we caught seemed a foot longer to everybody we showed them to.

There wasn't any swimming there for us though 'cause neither one had learned how yet. There were plenty that did at the nearby wide spot though since the Summers that close to Mobile were plain old HOT an' muggy like you wouldn't believe.

Me an' Ricky got a real shock a month or so later though. Intent on swimming in some muddy water near that spot, a couple of boys jumped in an' DIED.

Apparently they landed right on a big old boiling ball of Water Moccasins an' got bit maybe a dozen times each. I believe they'd both dropped right on a clutch

---

14

of those snakes mating an' swirling around in the water. The whole county was moved an' I tell you what it was, SNAKE SEASON for anybody with a gun, knife, or even a big rock for years after that.

We didn't know those boys or attend their funeral, but you can IMAGINE we got to looking at those snakes up in the trees. I knew there were Water Moccasins in the creek that fed the swimming hole, but would not for the life of me have guessed they were hanging around up in the trees! Ricky an' me looked at some pictures at school an' made one last trip back to our fishing spot for a good look. Sure enough they were Water Moccasins an' that was about the stone cold end of our favorite fishing spot.

A week or so later Daddy had finally gotten back from another long trip to Chicago an' the first thin' he wanted to do was go swimming! We all decided to walk down to another swimming spot (not too awful far from our private fishing hole) that had become one of the new favorites.

Daddy got in first an' took a turn around it just to check it out I guess. Then he yelled, "The waters fine! Come on in!" an' they did. It was quite a sight ta see all those cousins an' kin jumping in all at once.

There was flat out no way on God's green earth I was doing any swimming though. I was so hot I couldn't stand to watch everybody else get cooled off. Managing to talk a friend into loaning me an old inner tube, I finally did a tentative little bit' a floating for a

15

while. It was pretty peaceful too, so I 'bout fell asleep. Turns out my DADDY had other plans for me.

Hearing someone splashing toward me, half opening one eye, I saw daddy there with a big stick an' a little GRIN on his face. Since I hadn't learned to swim yet, my DADDY had decided that today was my DAY! He took that stick an' upended my inner-tube yelling out, "ALL RIGHT BOBBY! IT'S SINK OR SWIM SON!"

I could almost see that big ball' a swirling snakes, feel them closing on me with their fangs extending toward my bare flesh as my face hit the water. Flailing around in a vain attempt to push away the imaginary attackers, I managed to get my face above water an' was facing the opposite bank. Not seeing anyone or my inner-tube, I was really panicking now an' went under AGAIN.

Fighting my way back to the surface, I was facing toward Daddy an' could see he was coming my way with a concerned look on him. Then I was back in the dark, cold water.

Pushing every direction with all my strength, I managed to get an arm above the water an' felt a strong hand grab my wrist. Rising up into the sunlight, I sucked in a beautiful, sweet, deep, warm breath of summer air. Then my daddy was holding me an' wading back toward the shore.

He had about the sorriest look I'd ever seen on him as he set me down on the bank an' checked me over to make sure I was all right, wrapping a towel around my

---

shoulders as I shivered more with fear an' anxiety than cold, just glad to be outta the water an' outta reach' a those snakes.

Putting his arm around me then, Daddy didn't exactly apologize, but he let me know he'd prefer things'd gone a little different. I told him why I'd been so scared an' he nodded thoughtfully.

Then he said something I couldn't believe. It turns out he'd heard 'bout it an' was hoping that would help me get up on top' a the water! My head snapped around an' I fixed him with an open mouthed stare to make sure it was still my daddy sitting there!

That was the first I recall of many incredulous looks I gave people during my lifetime. It's just hard to believe what life goes on about sometimes.

Well me an' Ricky had a lot of fun, but what I had mostly at SCHOOL were TORMENTORS. Usually it was just that I got ignored or left out. There were plenty' a kids though, an' even grownups, that seemed to go outta their way to take a pot shot at me.

I remember in particular though Edward Voisard the third. That boy was the bane of the entire grade school. I was somewhere around twice as likely for trouble as I had the particular good fortune' a being the most natural target among his preferred herd' a victims.

The prevailing theory on his behavioral problems he shared with us little folks in the form of wedgies, wet willies, swirlies, an' the odd beating, was he was just

17

jealous 'cause we were all 'bout twice as smart as him in spite of him spending twice as long in about every grade he'd started. He'd been favoring the fifth grade for a couple of years at that point.

He was around thirteen an' pretty big to boot, with a wild black topknot an' a face that looked like it'd been squeezed together in a vice. I was pretty quick an' mostly managed to stay outta his way, but a confrontation was inevitable.

Finally, after a couple of months of the second grade, he cornered me in a dugout at the baseball field. I think he'd had a particularly bad day an'd been saving me up for it cause it was unusual for him not to want'n audience.

He sneered somethin'n' like, "Well if it ain't the littlest chicken turd on the lot!" warming up his whipping knuckles in the palm of his right hand, "You have a hard time suh-suh-suh-SAYIN' stuh-stuh-stuh-STUFF duh duh duh don't you!! Huh huh huh!" Mean folks just LOVED to do imitations of me, apparently for me to critique since it was mostly just in my presence.

Eddie did a pretty fair job, but as usual I had difficulty expressin' my appreciation. "You sh-sh-sh-sh-sh", I started AS a single tear rolled down my face. It always got worse when I was mad.

"Shut up?" he finished for me (that was another favorite pass time I got from some folks),"Nice comeback sh-sh-sh-SHITHEAD, now how 'bout some puh-puh-puh-PAYBACK?"

———

He came on ahead then, grinning a nasty snaggle toothed smile.

Kicking my legs an' whirling my fists, I tore into him the best I could, but he just held me off an' laughed for a couple of seconds, then served me upside the head like a TETHERBALL. I went down pretty hard.

He rolled me over, got his knees on my shoulders, an' started letting out a big old string' a spit right into my thrashing face. He'd let out satisfied grunts when he managed to get some in my MOUTH, that apparently being good for extra points. He slapped me a couple of times then an' laughed pretty good about that while I wailed at the whole world.

About that time he let out a grunt as his forehead smacked against the back wall' a the dugout.

Letting out a howl, he sprung off me, whirling around with both fists ready, kicking me in the head in the process. I was looking directly up into his crotch then an' saw the bottom of a familiar looking boot slam directly into it. Eddie let out a groan an' sunk to his knees while I rolled outta the way an' stood up.

I was face to face with my Uncle Roy an' my spirit SOARED!

"Well get out the way!" he insisted as he wound one up. I stepped aside an' he let it FLY. Even on his knees Eddie was only 'bout a head shorter than Roy, but Roy was just plain MEAN when he saw people kicking puppies or beating on me.

Eddies nose exploded all over my shirt an' he collapsed into the corner' a the dugout. "I'll kill you Roy Mizell!" he gurgled through the blood an' pain, cradling his busted up nose.

"You welcome to try Eddie," he calmly invited," but I'll be bringing a two by four next time." Eddies eyes widened a little at that 'cause he knew'e, Roy meant it. Roy was known to fight dirty for a good cause an' this about CEMENTED his reputation.

Roy threw an arm around my shoulder an' led me outta the dugout, wiping at my face with the tail of his shirt. "You all right Bobby?" he comforted me.

It was 'bout all I could do to snuffle without sobbing, but he understood. "Well," he went on, digging his knuckles into my head, "another couple of years you could take him yourself. You pretty wiry ya' know." I had to smile at that, an' I loved him right then more than anybody in the whole world!

We made our way back ta Grandpa's house. Grandma made a fuss over us, but didn't ask questions 'bout the blood on my shirt or the bruises on my face.

My Grandma was a good soul an' I loved her with all my heart, too. Roy seemed to take after her, I thought.

Whenever there was time, I'd be at her house having Chinaberry tea an' cookies. Just talking with an' being around her, was a childhood treasure that still shines for me. She always made me feel special, an' still does long after her death.

Grandpa came in 'bout then an' saw the condition I was in, an' Roy there with me. He wondered out loud if I'd been getting Roy in to my problems again. I could only look down at the floor.

Roy told him I hadn't done anything wrong, wishing out loud he'd leave me alone. Roy was like that, he'd just calmly say what was right an' leave it at that.

Grandpa didn't like that at ALL, "See what you do to my family boy? You've got my own son talking back to me, an' I won't have it!"

"Bu-bu-b-bu-but, G-g-gr-g-r-grampa I di-di-didn't d-do anyth-th-thin'!", I haltingly begged. He must'a had'a bad day or something, because he started raisin' his voice now.

"You know I EXPECT this sort of behavior from YOU. You're your father's boy an' he was a disobedient, back talking boy too, an' grew up into a NO GOOD man!" he finished.

I'd heard this sort of talk before an' I loved my father. I wasn't taking any more 'a that an' spoke up then! "M-m-my d-d-d-da-dads a g-g-good m-man!" I insisted, getting a little angry.

He got HOT at that, going on 'bout me not disrespecting him in his own home. Well, I guess he never saw his disrespect for my Daddy, but I guess it didn't matter much just then.

His favored form of corporal persuasion being the razor strap he kept on the wall of the kitchen, he snatched it off now an' grabbed my arm, dead set on tannin' my hide yet AGAIN.

Grandma had seen him strap me, for this before ,an' wasn't having any more I suppose. She earned another mark on Saint Peter's door post 'bout then an' FLEW TO MY RESCUE.

She knew I got picked on something awful, 'cause we'd sit an' talk 'bout it sometimes. She knew 'bout Roy's part too an' would encourage an' reward him behind Grandpa's back. Right about then, she lit into Grandpa with everything short of DIVORCE court!

Roy an' I both took a step back an' gaped at her when she up an' damned him for an old fool, just like THAT, grabbing at the strap in his hand.

"You let go woman, this boys goanna get some discipline his no good father never TOOK nor GIVES!", he demanded, giving that strap a shake, but she hung on like a terrier.

She got right in his face then, "You'll SIT your damn fool self right down an' LISTEN right now or you'll be COOKIN' your OWN damn meals an' SLEEPIN' IN THE SHED!!!" They stood locked in a test of wills for a moment. Her four foot eleven self pushing up ta her full height as Grandpa practically had to bend over to

—

22

look'er in the eye.

I'd never heard Grandma swear before an' even Grandpa looked shocked for a moment, then sat down slowly at the little kitchen table. Me an' Roy both just stood there with our mouths open, looking from one ta the other, wondering what had just happened.

She told him what had REALLY been going on, how the teachers an' kids treated me, an' how Roy stood up to impossible odds defending me when he got the chance. He actually started to tear up a little when he realized how he'd been persecuting me, too.

Roy piped in then telling him what had happened earlier. "I know you don't like it when I fight pa," he confessed, "but whenever I see people beating on Bobby I just can't help it. He's family even if you don't like John much."

Grandpa nodded then, an' tousled my head, dabbing at one of 'is eyes with 'is sleeve. "I had no idea Bobby.", he lamented, "an' I'm proud of you Roy!" He slapped Roy on the shoulder like a man. I'll say that's about the ONLY time I ever saw Grandpa back down from anything. That's when I knew Grandpa was a good man at heart, an' Grandma was a good an' STRONG woman.

A few weeks later I was suffering through yet ANOTHER bath. Mama insisted on personally scrubbing all the places a boy just couldn't stand for his mother to even SEE. I'm sure I was doing my usual job of resisting her with rolling eyes and the occasional exclamation of "M-m-m-mama!" along with my best salvo of squirming an' wriggling my soapy self any way I could.

There was some yelling from outside I recognized an' I peeked out the bathroom window to see Roy, his best friend Buddy Smith, an' Buddy's little brother Ronald all on bicycles, hollering for me to come on. It was about the end of the summer an' soon I'd be back at that hell of a school. I wasn't ABOUT to miss an opportunity to lay on another coat' a summer SWEAT an' DIRT if I could HELP it.

If I was disagreeable about being scrubbed before I became downright UNCOMPANIONABLE now in spite' a my mothers bi-weekly insistence at access to the backs' a my ears. She could see it was a losing battle at this point, giving me an "Oh all right then, go on!" an' I'm sure frowning at the half job she'd managed.

"T-t-t-tell them to w-wait mama!", I begged, toweling frantically at my chest an' legs as I hopped toward my room. Mama started downstairs to the porch to talk to them as hollering out a window was apparently too undignified for her. Actually, now that I think about it, that window probably got painted shut by a small boy in a hurry to get done that summer for a similar reason.

Throwing some clothes on my still damp body, I ran downstairs an' out the front door. They'd already started off, hollering back for me to catch up. Running to where my bike was leaning up against a tree, I didn't see what happened next, but I heard the noise.

—

A loud engine turning suddenly into sliding, scrabbling gravel, a truncated yell from Roy an' Ronald like no noise I'd heard them make before, an' we'd made plenty. There was a final sick crunch of metal, flesh, an' bone, I don't guess I'll ever forget.

Dropping my bike, I started slowly over to see, but my Mama got to me first. She wouldn't let me past, holding me so tight that breathing was hard. She sobbed an' yelled for my dad who was already out on the front porch running toward the noise.

When I finally managed to get a glimpse, I couldn't see Roy except for a hand sticking out from under the front bumper of a pickup. Buddy had been thrown all the way into somebody's yard about thirty feet away from Roy. Neither was moving. There was a twisted, broken bicycle in the middle of the road. Ronald had been knocked down an' was crying.

Dad was working on getting Roy out from under the truck, while a man who was obviously having a hard time staying upright even on his knees was trying to help. A neighbor had heard the commotion an' was doing what they could for Woodrow. My mother finally left me to help. She ran over to Ronald an' carried him into the house.

I walked slowly closer an' saw daddy still struggling to help Roy. He stopped then, slowly sitting back on his knees an' hanging 'is head.

Mama must' a sent for Grandpa 'cause he showed up

'bout then. Looking from my daddy to Roy's hand, he got on his knees an' reached out to 'is son under the truck. Standing up slowly, he steadied himself on the hood for a second, then saw that drunk swaying back an' forth, looking down at Roy's very still, small an' pale hand.

"GOD DAMN YOU!!" he roared. Now a hellfire an' brimstone preaching man understands that sort of talk an' he meant EVERY syllable. He was anxious to assist that fellow on 'is way to meet the well known provisionary of damnation as well. Launching himself at that fellow, he managed to knock him down before my father an' a neighbor could finally stop him. I think he would' a killed him.

I didn't care 'bout that though, he could a' killed that fellow a hundred times if it'd undo what I saw. My best friend an' protector, my hero, Roy Mizell was dead at the age of twelve. Buddy died too.

They were buried on a sunny day with the whole community in attendance. My seven year old mind expected them to get up outta their coffins an' play as I walked by what seemed to be their sleeping figures, napping in the Sunday clothes they hated so much.

Eddie even showed up at the funeral, an' he never bothered me again. I'm sure it's because he respected Roy. He'd saved me one last time as they lowered him into the ground.

When we got home that day, my bicycle was just GONE. When I asked about it Mama told me straight

---

up I was never touching a bicycle again as long as I
lived. I guess I didn't much care if I did either.

Roy's death seemed to take a lotta the fire outta
Grandpa. He just didn't seem the same after that. I
suppose he'd always thought Roy was the best thing
he'd ever done, an' I felt the same way.

One good thing that came from that was Grandpa an'
me got along a LOT better. He even decided he was
going to try to make a preacher outta me like he'd been
trying to do for Roy. I couldn't help but feel honored,
an' did my best to please, though I was scared to death
about talking in front' a people.

Grandma would scrub my face an' make sure my
clothes were just right on days when there was a prayer
meeting. It turned out not only did the whole
congregation just LOVE hearing me read the
scriptures, but for some reason I could talk when I read
the bible out loud. That was about a miracle in an' of
itself to everybody that knew me.

They even liked hearing me preach a little in my little
seven year old stuttering lisp. Grandpa would show
me off about every other meeting for a while an' all
those folks would shake my hand like I was Billy
Graham himself afterward!

In spite' a that I was sad for a long time after Roy died.
I didn't eat right, an' wouldn't go outside. Just trips
over ta Grandma an' Grandpa's house'n back. Even
Ricky Wallace couldn't get me to spend much time out

in the sun. He was a good friend though an' never stopped trying.

SHORTY

Sitting on the front porch one day, I watched Daddy come home with a box that had holes in it. Mama came out right away, drying her hands, "John..." she said in a warning tone, as she eyed the snuffling, scratching box.

"Now Mama," he interrupted, "…just wait.". I've got to say here, mama being who she is, I hadn't heard him give her too many "now mama's" so I knew SOMETHIN' was UP. He set the box down in front' a me an' waved me to it, putting 'is hands in his pockets an' even grinning a little. Now my Daddy hardly EVER smiled so I was a little EXCITED by then.

Looking in one of the holes I could see a baleful brown eye looking back at me. A blue spotted snout stuck out the side, whining an' licking.

Opening up the box, there looking up at me with a wagging tail was about the most mixed up half a blue tick mutt I'd ever SEEN. I tell you what it was love at first sight! I must' a been 'bout the smilin'est, happiest kid in the state of Alabama just then. I guess that's why mama never said another word.

I named him Shorty cause he turned out to be smallish, but he had a lotta heart! "Just like you Bobby!", Dad would say.

At first, we'd just play in the yard, but before ya' knew it, we were out in the woods together, running an' chasing after anything with four legs. I even got back on some vines, an' Shorty would bark like crazy while I went flying through the air.

Shorty got to where he would climb a tree even! It was about the craziest thing I ever saw, but it's the God's honest truth. He would wrap his front an' hind legs around any smallish tree he'd managed to run something up into, then sort of shuffle 'is way up.

He got as high as ten feet off the ground once. I'm sure any number of squirrels had a nervous breakdown when they saw that snarling snapping dog come climbing up after them! That's how it sounded anyway. That dog would wait for me outside school even!

He got pretty good about letting me chuck a slingshot rock at whatever he'd spotted before 'e took 'is turn, so we got to be a real hunting pair an' spent a lotta time in the woods around Grandpa's fifty or so acres of farm land.

Next year, my dad got me a single shot 22 rifle an' a box of short rifle shells an' I felt like a REAL mountain man then! Now I know you "modern" folks are thinking something like "Child abuse!" 'bout anybody that'd give a rifle to an eight year old, but that was pretty common stuff back then, an' I never heard of any accidental shooting's like you do now. Kids nowadays don't have any sense about guns because they learn 'bout them from damned old video games.

You might think I'd have got a little bloodthirsty shooting coons, squirrels 'an such, but the truth was I had a bit of a tender heart so young and the first time I ever really shot anything was about the last. Seems a little foolish I suppose, but that's how it was.

Well, once I'd got my rifle an' dog, I got to feeling just about brave anyway. Shorty an' me would spend the night in the woods around my Grandpa's farmland, even alone sometimes . Ricky Wallace would come along with us sometimes too, an' him'n me would get into what seemed like some pretty big adventures to us.

There was this time we were out at the school watching some kids play with one of those handle controlled model planes with a gas engine. That boy looked to us like he was having the time of 'is life, looping an' circling, while he went around an' around.

All of a sudden, the strings broke or come untied or something an' that plane TOOK OFF in to the woods! It went clean outta sight with about a dozen heart broke kids watching. I forget the boys name who lost it, but he was just about crying an' we all scattered trying to find it for a while without any luck.

That summer ALL the boys around my age tithed at least one day a week tramping around out there ta see if they could get at it. I'm betting they all were thinking "finders keepers" like me. Well…at least

30

some sort of permanent permission to fly it anyway. A lot of great days started with "Hey lets go see about that plane!" an' finished in a muddy scratched up mess that would make any boy grin.

It'd been a couple of months by now an' everybody had about given up when me an' Ricky decided to give it one last try. For some reason we figured since I had a rifle an' a dog that could climb a tree, an' Ricky could blow the biggest bubble in class, we had some particular advantage.

Well…we picked out a nice sunny day, loaded up on supplies an' water, then TOOK OFF. We got out further than I'd ever been out into a swampy spot that stank in the hot summer sun. It was a real tangle of moss covered trees an' broken up dead wood in a mushy muddy green bubbling mess…an' we LOVED it.
Pushing on through the stinking thick brush an' mud, Shorty started whining an' barking, hesitating down the trail a little bit. I whistled at him, calling for him, as I raised my leg to step over a log an' just STOPPED in mid-stride, just about striking a pose most people associate with a dog.

This particular log had two rows of spines an' looked a little scaly.

I'm guessing that alligator was around ten feet long, but whatever the size, I flat out HIGH TAILED it back up the trail, spraying a pretty good rooster tail' a mud. Shorty scrambled after me, trying to keep up, an' barking out what I'm sure was "I TRIED to tell you!"

Ricky stood there for a second hollering something at me when the brush started thrashing where that gator had been.

He passed me a second or two later.

I never told anybody 'cause I didn't want anybody calling me a chicken, but I guess Ricky must' a 'cause that story got around the neighborhood. That was the stone cold end of searching for that plane an' nobody said a thing to me.

Well one thing Daddy was always good for were surprises like Shorty. The next time he came back he had an even BIGGER box than the one Shorty had showed up in an' it even SMELLED new. Mama came in with a bird eating grin on her face, so I guess she knew what was up.

Daddy called us all in then carefully cut down the sides of the box. Letting the front fall down to the floor, we saw it for the first time…beautiful curved glass with wood trim, modern chrome highlights, space age buttons and knobs. We were in awe and stood in silence for a full ten seconds (a record in my household) gazing at the wonder Daddy had brought to us from far away places.

He'd got a television.

We only had radio before that an' we loved it, but it got plain old shoved aside when the TELEVISION showed up.

—

Well we dove right in to THAT. Mama liked some
daytime shows an' game shows. Daddy was in it for
the WRESTILIN', an he watched it like religion every
Friday with any friends or family that showed up.
ALL the kids liked about any cartoons that came on
an' "The Mickey Mouse Club" was a hit!

So I just about drowned in adventure shows and
cartoons for a while. Well naturally those shows
weren't just there for me. They wanted to SELL stuff
and son; they did a NUMBER on me! I wanted
everything those commercials said I should have.
When that announcer said "Kids! You've GOTTA
have it!" I just nodded my head.

Now I forget exactly what it was, but there was one at
the store, the man talking between the shows said I
HAD to have it, and It became my life's desire. I
believe it was a set of black cowboy gloves with real
leather fringe and somebody's famous name on the
back.

It wasn't just me either, just about every boy in the
neighborhood would go stand in the store and look at
those gloves. Son we were SMITTEN.

Well money being in short supply, I tried to talk mama
in to letting me do chores for money, but she wasn't
having any of THAT. She just went ON about how
SHE didn't get paid for any chores SHE did and son, I
thought I'd NEVER hear the end of it.

Well those hero's of mine kept saving the day every

—

33

week and that announcer kept insisting that I HAD to have those gloves if I was EVER going to be like THEM and I kept nodding my head. Before you know it one day I was in the store drooling over those gloves an' the next minute I just plain old WALKED OUT with them. Just like that!

Well I was just excited! I was going to be a real cowboy finally! I put them on an' went home, picking up any stick that looked like a gun on the way and making some very convincing recoil action to make the fringe fly on those gloves. I shot about a hundred imaginary bad guys on the way home and just had a GREAT time.

Until…

I got home and hid those gloves as long as I could. Mama had eyes in the back of her head though and could see through walls both I believe. So before you know it, I was suffering under the maternal inquisition and didn't have a single good answer for any question she had. I remember the end result though.

"Just you wait until your father gets home!"

Oh my.

Daddy being who he was (not having fell too far from Grandpa's tree) I was pretty certain that would only lead to tears, specifically MINE an' he didn't disappoint me at ALL on that score. Son he beat me so hard I couldn't sit down, AND he marched me back to that store and had me confess my deed and PAY UP!

Not having any money, I got to pay by sweeping dirt off the floor for a while. Other kids would wander by to chastise me an' enjoy my pain.

Well that FINALLY let up, but that announcer just wouldn't stop an' I HAD to get those gloves and a genuine fake imitation real plastic pearl handled cap gun to go with them.

Figuring there must be a better way to get a good toy, I picked up a few odd jobs. Mostly I walked around with Ricky sort' a acting as my business manager, asking old ladies if they needed lawns mowed, leaves raked an' whatnot. Then I'd do the work with Ricky helping some an' we'd split the money.

It turned out to be a fateful decision that led to an amazing change in my life!

One of the lawns I mowed was for a Mrs. Dunn. She could tell I didn't like to talk very much, an' the reason was obvious ever' time I opened my mouth, but it didn't bother her. She'd just smile gently an' wait patiently 'til I got my words out.

One day she invited me into her kitchen for some cookies. Well, consuming cookies was my specialty so naturally I consented.

Talking to me about school, she learned what I went through. I guess a cookie or two works better than Sodium Pentothal on a little boy an' I spilled my guts

---

in pretty short order 'round drinks of milk. She was the first adult outside my family that was any kind of interested in my problems, an' more than some 'a them!

It turned out that Mrs. Dunn was a retired teacher, an' not just any retired teacher. Would you believe it, she'd known other children with my problem an' had helped them!

You've got to remember there was NOTHIN' like a speech therapist or special education teacher back then in the South. It was just like my daddy said "Sink or swim!" an' this felt like striking gold to me! I might actually be able to talk like other kids?!

She came over to my house to talk to Mama 'n Daddy about it an' we all decided that I'd mow her lawn in exchange for lessons. I was glad to do it! Sitting in her living room, I'd read out loud, or she patiently ran me through drill after drill until I got it, gently correcting me when I didn't.

She NEVER made me feel bad when I couldn't get it right. We'd just stop for cookies or I'd go play, then I'd try again later. I'd improved a lot by the end of summer (an' gained a few pounds besides).

Next school year I wasn't even the same boy! Kids an' teachers both started treating me better. I went out for sports in the church leagues, an' I even started talking to GIRLS! I knew I'd been alive for a while, but it felt like that's when my life started.

Of course this meant Ricky wasn't my business

———

manager any more an' I got to keep all the fruits of my own labor, a benefit of speech I hadn't conceived of. A light went on in my head for sure then. I'd discovered the value of education an' I can see now where it saved my life on a number of occasions.

The first day I knew I could speak, I mean really knew I could speak, me an' Shorty went ta the general store with fifty cents I'd earned an' just asked for whatever I wanted. Candy mostly, an' a comic book, I think. Going out on the boardwalk then, I asked one of those old fellows there to play a game of checkers an' just talked about the weather, ate candy, an' looked at my comic book.

I was free! It was about the best day of my young life.

Mrs. Dunn is another treasure from my past that I'll never forget an' can't thank enough. I'll pay her the highest compliment I know how to give for the whole world to see. She was the first person in my life outside of family that I knew for sure was a child of God. I'm certain if there's a heaven she's in it!

My new found confidence even led to me planning my first real solo adventure.

Robbers Roost was a hollow down the road a piece with an unsavory reputation of the sort that everybody loved to talk 'bout, but nobody wanted to confess to. Word was that thieves, moon shiners, hucksters, hobos, an' dark figures of all sorts wondered those woods running either to or from trouble, so naturally it had a real draw for a boy with something to prove.

—

Picking out a good Saturday, I got up early so there wouldn't be to many questions. I'd learned something 'bout getting into trouble by now, so I packed up the necessities. My rifle, an old canteen, an old WW11 cargo pack filled with sandwiches (Shorty was partial to egg salad), extra ammunition, a trusty pocket knife, an' of course Shorty himself rounded out the support team.

I slipped out the back door, shushing Shorty to stop his whining an' sniffing at the pack, an' we were off! Running as fast as I could, we got outta earshot before Mama could start hollering. There was nothing that got a hold of my spine more than her yelling a dire threat if I didn't show up pronto.

I'd decided to cut across some fields so nobody would see what I was up too. It wasn't terribly unusual to see a young boy with a gun hiking out into the woods back then, but it might draw attention an' I didn't want my parents knowing where I'd gone. Feeling like I'd covered just about everything, I was feeling pretty confident, an' even started whistling as we got closer.

Starting into the big gully where I'd been told it all happened, the whistling stopped under the weight of reality. It seemed like a good idea to be quiet at this point.

Well it turned out it might have been a pretty hot spot at one time, but I didn't find much. Just an old abandoned still or two, an' some trails. The most interesting thing I discovered was on the way out.

———

Deciding to go home, I wasn't too worried about people seeing me do that so I just headed toward the road. Just as I'd got up the road a ways, I heard a truck coming by an' figured I'd better hide anyway. Skittering up a little rise into some foliage, I hid an' waited.

Son was I surprised to see one of the Sherriff's trucks driving by with a deputy standing up in the bed with a shotgun! Most surprising of all was the contents of the truck! Not that I'd drunk any moonshine myself, but it was as clear as day what the clear liquid in those boxes of unlabeled gallon jugs was!

Maybe I'd got up into the wrong gully, but if I had it was my lucky day. I'm not for sure WHAT would've happened if they'd caught me sniffing around where I shouldn't, with a gun.

There was no way I wanted any Sherriff's deputies, or for all I knew the Sheriff himself, thinking I might spill the beans anyway (or corn I guess in this case). I decided to high tail it outta there through the thickest brush I could find.

I supposed it was possible they'd made a raid of some kind. Stories like that usually ran around our little bump in the road like wildfire. A week or two passed an' I still hadn't heard anything. I wasn't for sure what they were up to, but I was smart enough not ta tell ANYBODY about that for decades. Not until long after even Shorty was dead.

—

Well there were a number of confidence building'
episodes like that. So by the time school had come
around again I'd pretty well come outta my shell an'
had some friends besides Ricky even! The teachers
had stopped slapping me, Eddie had stopped whaling
on me, an' I'd got me a little respect.

Most of my friends were white boys, but for some
reason I had more black friends than most of the other
boys. I reckon because they understood a little better
what it was like to get looked down so they hadn't
picked on me or shunned me so much because of my
speech. I don't remember any white boys that didn't
have a black friend or two though, an' we all seemed to
get on pretty well in school to me.

The black family that my Grandpa shared his land with
had children 'bout our age an' we'd play with them too.
I went to school with a couple of them also an' they
seemed pretty decent to me. One of them named
Joseph was about my age an' we were in school
together that year.

One school day a busload of black folks rolled into
town an' parked in front of the school with a big sign
on the side that said "NAACP: We Shall Overcome!"
Joseph an' me stood at the window watching while
they started marching around in front of the school
with signs about "We protest school segregation!" an'
"Don't treat our children like PRISONERS!", or some

———

such.

Me an' Joseph crowded up to the window with all the other kids. We looked at them an' back at each other, trying to figure what they were all about. The sheriff an' some deputies showed up then an' we had a real circus! It looked like they were just there ta enjoy the show cause all they did was watch.

Some of the protesters yelled at the Sheriffs, but they just laughed. I understand there were some places where the police beat on these folks, but none of that happened here, that I saw or heard of.

The teacher shooed us away from the windows an' back to our seats. We did our best to ignore the excitement outside an' pay attention to our lessons, but I'm afraid that day was a write-off for our little communities' educational history. When the bell rang an' we all ran out you should' a seen the look on those fellows. I guess nobody from their bunch had bothered to actually look in the school before they got all freedom marching on us.

Some folks will say the whole South, around 1960 ,was like a race riot in Birmingham, with the National Guard, marching colored kids, into hate filled racist schools, desperately in need of integration, but that just wasn't so, not where the blacktop ended anyway. I'm not saying everything there was perfect, 'cause nothing is. It just wasn't like that where I grew up.

Would you believe it, the next day the KKK showed up in some trucks; sheets, cone hats, an' all! They

—

were carrying signs to 'bout "racial purity" an' "Don't push our children out!"

Frankly some of the stuff they were yelling back an' forth didn't make it seem like either group was much interested in what was best for children. Those KKK boys had 'bout the same reaction when school let out though.

Both groups went around for a few days trying to get people in our little community to act up with them, but it seemed like nobody was having any of either. I remember my dad saying to one of those KKK boys, "Well we can see you went to a lot of trouble, but the fact is we just aren't interested."

Seemed to me like Josephs dad felt the same way. He still let us play together, an' his dad an' mine would just look at the ground an' shake their heads when they'd stand together talking.

Then came the night the KKK burned a cross right there in front of the school. Some folks came out to see it, black as well as white. The glow of the fire flickered on my bedroom window a half mile away.

I guess neither side felt that drew the kind of crowd they wanted cause they all packed up an' left shortly after. Near as I could tell the whole community breathed a collective sigh of relief.

My Uncle Dan was pretty hot headed, but even he wasn't buying into those KKK folks though. I liked my Uncle Dan, in spite of him not being what my

Grandpa had in mind. He was still at home after Roy died an' I think Grandpa still had a hope of getting a preacher from one of his own sons. I'll spoil the suspense here an' say it didn't work out with Dan.

He knew what Roy had been doing for me an' had done his best to fill in where he could until Mrs. Dunn had cured me. He was a Senior in high school by then, 'bout six foot, pretty athletic, an' strong willed.

One day I went with him to the hardware store an' somehow we ended up at the Moose lodge. He was supposed to get me back in time for Grandpa's prayer meeting but we ended up being there a little longer than wisdom liked.

The rules were a little looser back then so I wound up sitting near the bar, watching him put away a pretty sizable quantity of beer an' the odd shot of whatever. The Moose lodge doubled as the nearest gentlemen's watering hole if you didn't count the stills I'd heard 'bout up the road at Robbers Roost.

The lodge didn't require membership for drinking so you got a pretty mixed crowd in there. I remember that day there were redneck farmers, military men, loggers, an' some other locals. Somebody must' a said the wrong thing to somebody 'cause there was some shouting an' before I knew it 'bout half that crowd was laying into each other while the other half scattered or took bets.

Fists, chairs, an' bottles were flying every which way an' Uncle Dan was right in the middle of it! That old bartender busted out a Louisville Slugger an' lit into some of the worst ones, including my Uncle, but it didn't do much good.

Well, my part in this play seemed dubious to me, so I lit out for the door. Before I could get there a couple of fellows rumbled into my path just whaling on each other. That big farmer knocked a sailor right out from under his beamy then whirled around with those ham sized fists cocked…an' there I was.

That was 'bout the brawniest old redneck I'd ever laid eye's on an' my little ten year old brain figured he was about to lay into me next. He just snorted like a freight train, grabbed me, an' threw me out a broken window into the dirt outside. I realize now he was just doing me a favor, but I felt like I'd been through a knock down drag out brawl at the time.

Uncle Dan came staggering out a little later an' sat down on the ground next to me. His head hung down for a minute then he looked over at me with a smile on his bloody face. "Well now that was something wasn't it?" he said, an' started laughing.

We got up an' walked to Grandpa's house where Dan still lived. My Uncle was not in any kind of shape you'd call good an' he probably smelled like a still too.

Grandpa's prayer meeting was already underway an' they were hollering an' shouting. There was a curtain he put up so folks couldn't see the kitchen which suited my Uncle just fine, since he was trying to sneak by into his bedroom.

———

44

I could see Grandpa, silhouetted on the curtain against the light in the living room. His arms were spread wide an' he'd just put some exceptional high eloquence on a particularly fiery description of the depths of hell that had raised a fine response from his congregation. He paused for a moment to wind up for the next run, in a state of high ecclesiastical form an' ecstasy, when Dan bumped against a wall decoration.

Grandpa turned, pulled the curtain back, an' there was the whole congregation an' my Gran'father looking at my Uncle as he did his best to stand his drunk, beat up self straight an' still as he could. "Ummm...hey." was the best he could manage.

The bouquet of his breath reached my Gran'father an' I could see his mouth snap shut an' his eye's widen as he realized where my Uncle had taken me, an' more or less what had happened I'm sure.

Grandpa was a big man that worked hard. I started feeling sorry for my Uncle Dan as soon as I saw him make a fist. He laid out Dan so hard his head cracked the plaster as it bounced off the wall.

Grabbing his razor strap off the kitchen wall, he came back at Dan as he crawled down the hall. Letting loose a roaring soliloquy of hellfire an' brimstone he'd already wound up for, an' that strap to boot, he laid into Dan two mighty blows. Raisin' it for a third time, he paused for some reason.

It all just went outta him then. His shoulders slumped,

his head fell, an' the strap dropped to his side. Dan made it into his room an' shut the door. That living room was quiet as a tomb for a full New York minute.

"AMEN!", hollered one of the men in the small congregation. Grandpa turned slowly an' let the strap fall to the floor. "Amen.", he muttered quietly. "You'd better go on home Bobby." he said quietly to me as he returned to his podium, an' slowly shut the curtain. I heard him begin on a quieter track on his sermon as I slipped out the back door.

Dan left home an' joined the military inside of two weeks. It seemed like how our Grandpa's entire family started their own lives.

Now all this time I'd been attending my Grandpa's church meeting's EVERY Sunday. Since he'd try'd to make a preacher out of me I'd come to appreciate what he did and was anxious to meet 'is expectations. I learned to love listening to him go on about the depths of Hell and the love of God, and of course how much Jesus loved us.

One day in particular my Grandfather had finished up a sermon about "love they neighbor" and "charity faileth not" and so on. I'd listened the whole time, proud to be his Grandson and hanging on every word.

Well I walked home with him and Grandma and was sitting in the kitchen when Grandpa came BUSTIN' in from outside! His face was red and he looked at me like I'd kicked him in the rear!

Grabbing my arm, he accused me of stealing some tool of his!

I said I was innocent, but it didn't matter, he'd already made up his mind. Maybe he'd heard about the gloves, I don't know.

Grandma gave him a stern "Now Grandpa!", but he wasn't after my hide this time. He just wound up and let out all the HELLFIRE and BRIMSTONE he hadn't got to preach today and let me know in no uncertain terms exactly where I was GOIN' and what it was goanna be LIKE!

I just couldn't believe it! After him going on for a full hour about charity and loving, I KNEW I hadn't taken that tool though and I wasn't having any this time.

Shaking loose of his grip, I just left. I shook with rage and a swearing under my breath all the way home, that I'd never set foot in his house again!

And I didn't either for almost two years. I learned to rely on my friends more during that time.

Now like I said before, the Army, Navy, Marines, an' Air Force. All Grandpa's boys left home a little different. The thing we all had in common though…was football.

Grandpa's boys were all pretty big, an' the one thing they ALL managed to do that made him happy was

---

football. In Alabama football is just about a religion. Bear Bryant was the second coming an' Denny-Bryant stadium was the Vatican. It was the one thing I could tell Grandpa an' Dad still had in common.

I liked football well enough, but those big old boys slamming into each other seemed more like something I'd rather watch than feel. I was in high school by then and my Daddy had different ideas about that.

If I'd tried out for the team on my own they'd have probably given me a short speech 'bout perseverance an' grit then cut me loose, but my dad knew the coach. That was the start of some trouble for me.

The coaches name was Dane Miller an' my Dad buttered his bread up on both sides talking 'bout how fast I could run an' how wiry I was. The long an' short of it was inside of a month, I was the only hundred an' five pound linebacker on the field. The pads were 'bout two sizes too big, but there I was anyway.

I showed up for the practices, an' did my level best not to make a liar outta my dad. He'd told the truth, but I was 'bout five foot nothing an' like I said only a touch over a hundred pounds. Fair to say I got pushed around a little, but I showed plenty' a fire so they let me stay.

They even took enough of a shine to me that they provided the honor of a thoroughly humiliating initiation.

We all showered after practice an' girls hung around

outside the gym waiting on current an' potential boyfriends, neither of which I felt qualified to be. I wasn't sure what was going on when they grabbed me outta the shower, but it was more than a little embarrassing when they dumped me butt naked outside the gym door right in front of all the cutest girls that little school had to offer!

They wouldn't let me back in either, so I ran a half mile home naked as a jay bird. Fortunately, there was plenty of honking an' hollering to encourage what's probably safe to say was my record sprint to the house.

That was something they did to everybody that made the team so I didn't take it personal since it meant I was "in" (which was good). I guess maybe I showed too much spunk though 'cause they put me on the first string starters as a linebacker for reasons I have as yet to fathom, an' my first game was that Saturday night.

Dutifully lining up, I found myself staring at the knee's of one of those big old farm boys they make out there in the sticks. By the time I'd worked my way up to his eye's he'd developed a wicked grin. "I'm goanna mush you up son.", he muttered without a trace of regret.

There wasn't much I could say to that. Truth hurts I hear, or was about to anyway near as I could figure.

Well it could be truthfully said he pretty much ran over me any number' a times. The one time I DID get the ball him an' about six more, I couldn't tell apart piled on me like black on a tire. I tell you what, it flat hurt

---

49

an' the silver lining on that cloud just went clean OUT. When I was finally able to get up, I just walked off the field, shedding pads as I went, walking out the gate an' on to the house. The cheering an' noise drifted into my bedroom window where I lay an' groaned until it was all over.

I was still laying there when my dad finally came up an' looked in on me. "Rough night?" was all he said. All I could do was nod.

"Well," he drawled, "you gave it a damn good try." He closed the door an' walked away.

My heart swelled up an' I just about started crying I was so happy. My dad was proud of me! That was the first time in my life he'd ever spoken to me like a man too. Suddenly it had all been worth it. My football career was short, but very fulfilling!

I still liked sports an' was a pretty fair hand at anything that a pitch, sprint, or swing would get you through. I suppose football will always have a special place in my heart though, because it took everything I could give it, an' I gave it everything I had. Mind you I never set foot on anybodies gridiron ever again since I valued my life.

Dad had put a spark in me though. (The one that lights a fire to grow up an' act like a man) I started shaving any suspected whisker I could even imagine popping outta my baby smooth chin, putting on after shave, an' even talking to girls. Of course when you started talking to girls, there was one accessory that was the ultimate tool of the trade...a CAR.

I was only fourteen at the time, but I got plain old car
CRAZY! Maybe being deprived of a bicycle made me
want it all the more.

When I asked my mom an' dad 'bout it I remember my
Dad saying, "If you can buy one an' make it run, I
reckon I'll sign off on a license."

I'm sure they thought that'd be the end of it since
employment wasn't exactly plentiful or high paying for
young fellows in that neck of the woods.

We had four acres though, so I decided I was goanna
try my hand at farming! I worked my fingers right
down to the bloody bone with hoeing, raking, planting,
an' weeding. Every night I'd put myself to sleep
counting bushels an' dreaming 'bout my car.

One day my momma just up, an' decided she wanted
the fruits of my labor, an' TOOK it. Thinking back on
it, I suppose she was about as anxious for me to drive a
car as she'd been for me to ride a bike.

Dad was gone to Detroit for a month so there was
nobody to take my side, an' I admit to being a little bit
scared 'a my mama. I figured I ate the food anyway so
I just went with it, but that only increased my desire
for some green crispy MONEY!

A few weeks later I shocked them both by managing to
get my first real job cleaning up at a cabinet shop, an'
my fathers words burned in my heart. A car was what

—

51

I craved an' license or no, I was going to keep my end of the bargain I'm sure he thought he hadn't made.

I managed to save up twenty five dollars before I turned fifteen an' got me a CAR! Whatever you're imagining I got for that kind of money, you're probably right.

It was a 1952 Aero Willys. The Willys company made a pretty fair product that, from my experience with my first car, lasted a little longer than it had a right to. It was a Willys though an' had the same name stamped in the metal that the legendary WWII jeeps did. It felt like owning a piece of history! It seemed about that old to me anyway.

One of my Uncles an' me put a fair amount of knuckle scraping, scrounging, begging, an' plain old sweat into that rusty beast. A week or so later he was under the hood yelling at me to "Try it again!" an' it actually sputtered ta life for a couple of seconds an' I was HOOKED. It sputtered, ground, an' shook like it was talking to me. That car an' me had a few conversations that weren't entirely devoid of expletives as I recall.

The more we poked, tightened, bled, an' swore, the longer it seemed to want to talk. Finally my Uncle, Ricky Wallace, another one of our buddies, an' me were standing around watching the engine try to shake itself off the rusty motor mounts with tremendous satisfaction.

Then Ricky piped up, "Hey why don't we take it for a drive!" I had to scratch my head a little at that one.

"Well," I demurred, "We just barely got her running."

"Well how are you goanna know what's working if you don't give her a try?", he grinned.

I must' a frowned at that point cause he went ahead an' drove the last nail in that particular coffin by adding, "Besides, your mom an' dad are gone, who's goanna know?"

Between what seemed to me like Ricky's irrefutable logic, an' my desperation to whiz down the road, my common sense didn't stand a chance. We piled in an' before you knew it there was a plume of dust following us around the dirt roads!

We whooped, honked, an' generally made a fool of ourselves. Fortunately, we were on a long straightaway when I figured out she was long on go an' a little short on stop, but we got that fixed too.

After a while, Shorty got tired of being left behind an' jumped in with us one day. Seeing him throwing his tongue out the side an' enjoy the wind in his nose added a whole new pleasure to driving.

That old Willys wasn't much to brag 'bout on it's best day, but I did anyway. As will happen when you go on about something you shouldn't, lo an' behold somebody double dog dared me to PROVE it would run.

"Well...ummm.." was the best protest I could come up

---

with. "I thought so Mizell!" one of those high school boys spit at me, "You're a plain old LIAR!"

I straightened up a little at that, "Well I guess you're gonna see her run then!" I promised, immediately regretting my words.

Figuring a football game up the road at the school was the least dangerous distance for my lisenceless, under-aged self to drive an' the best venue ta show off my "classic", my destiny was set. I picked a night when mama was at some friends an' daddy was outta town.

I pushed it away from the house some, so nobody would hear it start. I was still what you'd have to fairly say was the runt of the litter, so I had to stack two pillows on the seat an' stretch my neck ta see over the dashboard.

The lights an' cheering in the distance seemed a lot farther, an' the car a lot noisier than usual as I drove her down the street. Whipping the wheel frantically back an' forth across the foot wide gap in the steering to keep her between the lines, I somehow managed to get into a double wide parking spot outside the fence with a pretty good view of the field.

I posed up on the hood in my best jeans an' clean white t-shirt while some fellows who'd seen me pull up sauntered over for a look. We talked cars between whistles, while the home team took a beating.

Then came the question I was dreading, "So what's under the hood?" Well I knew what was under the hood, an' I wasn't entirely sure bailing wire an' chewing gum would make my reputation as a mechanical genius. Still, I dutifully raised the lid for their appraising stares. "Huh..." was 'bout the best compliment I got on my efforts there.

"Well..." Ricky finally broke the silence,"...she runs!" They all nodded. There was no denying it now. Turned out my audience was fairly impressed, but it was NOTHIN' compared to the interest the police that had pulled up an' parked nearby seemed to take.

The game wore on an' the stares of those cops seemed to bore into the back of my head. The final play ended, the whistles sounded, an' everybody started leaving but me an' those cops.

Weighing the chances of them believing I was a midget that forgot his license an' registration, I did my best to act like a man that didn't have a car an' decided a nice walk home was just what I needed.

I'm supposing you might be able to imagine the scene when my parents discovered the car missing. You'd have thought it'd be a while before me or the Willys had any more adventures. It's funny though how things happen sometimes.

The house was dark when I got home. Breathing a sigh of relief I slipped through the front door, closing an' locking it behind me. Turning to go up the stairs, a lamp came on an' there was my mama sitting on a rocking chair facing the door.

——

55

I jumped three feet off the floor an' just about wet myself, but I was about as caught as you can get.

It didn't take much for her to get the truth outta me, since I was raised with a healthy fear of very few people an' God, Mama, an' Daddy were on the short list. Mama managed to get at the top of that last more than her fair share I think. She fixed me with "the eye" an' I spilled the beans.

Figuring I was 'bout to be beat to within an inch of my life, I just stood there, looking at the ground an' waited for it. Nothing happened for a few minutes, so I finally looked up at her.

The expression on her face was mostly anger, but there was a kind of thoughtful look there an' she was nodding slowly. I flinched a little when she opened her mouth, expecting the worst, but all she said was "You can drive?"

Now I wasn't expecting that. "Well…yes ma'am." was all I could say to that. Then I waited for the other boot to drop right on me. She considered that for a minute or two an' her expression changed into something that made me nervous. "Now isn't that something.", she finally said an' shooed me up to my room.

My mama took a real interest in my car after that. At first I though she was impressed with how grown up I was. She wasn't mad at me or anything, but I didn't much like the gleam in her eye.

—

Figuring out what it was happened a few days later
when she started ordering me up for transportation. I'd
never thought about it before, but I realized then,
mama had never been taught how to drive!

Before you knew it I was her personal driver! Mama
had me hauling her to the store, to the salon, to friend's
houses, an' church meetings. It was pretty fun at first,
but I got tired pretty quick of sitting outside her
friend's houses for hours at a time.

About the third time I sat an' watched her try on
dresses on a Saturday afternoon, I just 'bout regretted
ever seeing that old car. I didn't dare say anything
about it though, 'cause I wasn't much interested in
finding out how daddy felt about the whole situation or
getting on my mama's bad side either one.

A few months of that cut into my social life enough
that I was about ready to tell daddy myself though.
He'd come home from another trip an' we were all
having dinner together. We ate an' I stewed about how
I was going to tell him I didn't want any more driving,
instead of begging to get a license like most fifteen
year olds.

I guess mama could tell I was about ready to quit the
limousine business. She'd gotten real confident in my
driving too, I guess 'cause she up an' told daddy all
about it herself then. The way she told it I was a first
class, black tie chauffer. Daddy looked a little
surprised, but with mama on my side all he said was

"Well my son the driving man!", an' smiled as 'e dug back into 'is green beans.

Mama even eased up enough for me to have the car to myself some an' things got better. Oh, there was still some chauffeuring to do, but she'd let me go about where I wanted around town an' that was all right with me!

Feeling free and easy like that, I even drove over ta Grandpa's house and apologized for running off. Grandpa surprised me right back by doing some apologizing' his own self!

"Bobby..." he started slowly, "...people do foolish things sometimes, even good people. Just forgive and forget, that's the only way to get by so I tell ya what. You forgive me for being a damned old fool sometimes, and I'll forgive you just anytime you need forgiving. How 'bout that?"

Well that sounded just fine to me! We gave each other a BIG hug then and he told me he loved me. I think what happened is he found that tool laying around somewhere, but I didn't care. I was just happy to have my Grandpa back!

That didn't last long though, only a month or so later after a long day of preaching, Grandpa just up and had a Heart Attack in his big stuffed chair in the living room.   He was rushed to the doctors office, but died within a little while. We all held Grandma at the funeral while she cried and for weeks afterwards too.

I'd always thought a lot of my Grandpa, but I had no

—

idea how the county felt until I saw that funeral! There must have been THOUSANDS of people at his grave the day they buried him! Looking around at all those faces, hearing their whispered prayers for his family, I knew I wanted to do everything I could to be that kind of man.

Going up the path to Grandma's house came natural to me again, but now I was going for her. Now we'd talk about Grandpa and I'd make her tea and bring cookies and bread from Mama, then just sit and listen.

A LOTTA things were beginning to change that fall though. State surveyors came through town with fancy looking instruments. The word' a the day was "easement". They were supposedly trying to figure out just how much of us the state owned so they could do something, an' that something was finish a highway all the way to the Louisiana border along route 5 right in front of our house!

Well, a lot of folks thought that was just great. More business, growth, an' folks zooming back'n forth in front of our house. I didn't know a lot, but I knew things changed. I'd changed for the better, so I supposed this change could be for the better too.

Sure enough, along came the paving crews with their graders, steam rollers, an' dump trucks laying down a base for the new road. They built us a real first class drainage system too. The whole thing was a real production us kids would go watch!

Before you know it the smell of tar filled the air an'

stank for a long time through any open window. Some called it the smell of civilization, but not everybody could convince themselves it was sweet. The old timers in front of the store were about evenly divided on it.

Shorty didn't seem to appreciate it too much. He'd stay in the back yard, only coming out to bark at those chain gangs they used for shovel work, or any machines that got to close to what was his. If I insisted he'd come with me an' do the same, while I sat an' watched the machines grade, crush, an' flatten their way through the middle' a town.

Mama said I'd better shut him up, but I trusted Shorty an' let him have his say. The entire "road circus" had a vaguely bullying air about it, which the whole town seemed ta retreat from an' Shorty was ready to FIGHT!

I tell you what though, they laid down the slickest bran' new black road we EVER saw. When the paint crews came through an' put down the lines it really looked like something to us. Our only guide for driving down Main Street up till then had been the dust clouds from other cars.

It occurred to me only to late that this wonderful road might be the last nail in the coffin of my driving. The peace an' plodding pace of a dirt road had been a friend I was about to start missing.

Turns out the law takes driving on the blacktop a lot more seriously than dirt roads. I couldn't even hope to drive much by myself anymore, but could only watch jealously as adults in shiny new cars, an' rusty old ones like mine, surged back an' forth going wherever they wanted when they wanted. It just didn't seem fair to me or the old Willys that mostly just sat gathering rust now.

Shorty seemed to take my side like always an' keep fighting that road, chasing any car that slowed down a little. A lot of dogs in town did. My Uncles an' Dad would all say, "You better keep Shorty outta the road!" an' I'd go shoo him off, but he'd be back at it again.

A year after they'd got that road finished through town an' beyond to parts unknown, Uncle Leslie came into the house one day an' said simply "Bobby, you better go get Shorty outta the road." I went out to shoo him off one more time. He was taking a nap next to the road.

I hollered for him to come an' got yelps of panic an' pain for my trouble. I knew immediately what had happened an' ran to kneel over him. Blood was coming outta his mouth an' he was trembling.

He'd howl when I touched him, but I picked 'im up anyway an' let 'im bite at me. I deserved it, needed it to make me feel better. I hadn't kept him outta that road an' now one of those city fools had smashed up my best friend. For all I knew they'd done it on purpose too.

Dad wasn't in town an' it wouldn't have mattered if he was anyway, since there was no Veterinarian. Even if there had been we wouldn't't've had the money for it.

—

61

Putting' 'him on a blanket on the back porch, I frantically bandaged what I could, but Shorty still wouldn't do anything, but howl an' bite at me. Nothing' I did stopped the blood coming' outta his mouth either. It was terrible to listen to 'him screaming' in pain like that, but I didn't know what to do.

I felt a gentle hand on my shoulder, an' I turned ta see my Uncle Leslie with a pained expression on his face. He was carrying my 22 rifle. "Let's take him out in the yard Bobby." he almost whispered.

Knowing what he was about, I'm sure I put up a fight. "No! I...I could bandage him some more! We could give him some time!" I frantically insisted. Grasping desperately at any straw, but the one I knew was the inevitable last.

I'd started some watermelons that year in the best spot I could find, an' the vines had grown thick an' fast. Shorty loved to take naps under those shady vines in the cool damp dirt of my garden. Taking corners of the blanket we carried him as careful as we could an' set him down in his favorite spot. Loading' the rifle, Uncle Leslie lifted it to 'is shoulder while I cried.

He was about to squeeze the trigger when I reached out 'an pulled the barrel down. Leslie looked me in the eyes for a second. Shorty was quieter now, still whimpering' his pain. Leslie handed me the rifle then, but I could hardly imagine what to do with it for a minute.

—

"I'm so sorry Shorty. I'm sorry. I'm…" I couldn't speak anymore. Tears clouded my eyes until I couldn't see 'him anymore. Wiping' away the tears, I could see those brown eyes looking' at me with all the trust in the world.

I remembered seeing' 'him for the first time through the holes in that box an' a thousand other times I'd told him all my problems. Talking to 'him again, for the last time, I explained the situation the best way I knew how, talking until I felt like he understood.

Putting' the barrel against 'is head then, I closed my eyes. He was running' with me now, sleeping' at the foot 'a my bed when he was a puppy. I laughed as he shuffled his way up a tree the first time. We sat at a fishing' hole together.

"I love you Shorty. " The trigger seemed to pull itself this time.

For the second time in my life, my best friend in the whole world was dead. I guess that's progress.

We buried him under those watermelon vines.

Grandma said Shorty was just about definitely a Heaven bound animal if there ever was one an' even quoted a Bible verse to me 'bout a dog. There was a sinner of some sort needing a miracle from the Savior. He said, "It's not meat for dogs to eat the bread of the children." She replied, "Yes Lord, but even dogs eat the crumbs that fall from their masters table."

She got her miracle.

I still like to think of Shorty that way. Waiting' patiently at the Lords table for a crumb to fall, just like he did at ours.

That made me feel better, so I guess I got my miracle too.

When Daddy finally came home he went out back and stood by the grave with me for a while and pronounced his own blessing', simply saying "He was a good dog."

My father had always kept pretty busy between working at the airbase an' having' seven other kids, so it was a real treat to have any time alone with him.

He must' a figured I needed something' special after Shorty died cause he showed some real courage a month or so later by agreeing' to drive us both to Dolphin Island in my car to see what we could hook an' cook.

I can count on one hand the number of fishing' trips we took together, an' they were all wonderful, but I remember the one to Dolphin Island the best. It was a beautiful day an' my dad actually smiled, which was just about another miracle, as we hit the blacktop headed South.

We got the Willys up to 'bout fifty five miles an hour an' it started vibrating' so we slowed down a little an' just soaked in some sun. Other cars honked an' a few people shared a thought as they zoomed past.

We'd got to talking' 'bout the best fishing' spots when my dad noticed a tire rolling' by. "Would you look at that, some fool lost a lug nut!" he chided, slapping' me on the leg to get my attention. I'd worked on the car getting' it ready for the trip recently an' hesitantly informed him that the tire looked familiar.

He slapped both hands on the steering' wheel an' sat bolt upright. I grabbed the dashboard an' held on while he slowly pulled the car over to the side' a the road. It took about fifteen minutes to find the tire.

Borrowing' some lug nuts from the other tires, we got it back on.   It's fair to say we put some effort into the tightening' aspect of the operation. "Ya' know son," he advised, putting' his hand on my shoulder as I bore down on that lug wrench for about the twelfth time on one nut, "it might be best if we didn't bother your mother about this."

I was pretty glad he felt that way, cause I know I did. We went on to the island anyway an' had a great time! That trip alone was worth all the work, money, an' blood I'd put into that old Willys.

My life was about what I wanted it to be then. High school was pretty good. While actual popularity had eluded me, I had friends. A reasonable number of girls I thought were cute would talk to me. Nobody groaned when it was my turn ta bat or play third base. I even had a car!

The fix was in for the next few years as far as I was concerned.

To top it off, the next weekend daddy did something' unheard of in my short lifetime. He up an' invited me out for dinner at the burger joint up the road. Just me an' him, an' he even let me drive!

I needed exactly one finger to count the number of times that ever happened. It was a seriously big deal an' I knew something' was up. At first I figured he wanted to talk to me about college, but I remembered him an' mama had been arguing' a lot more than usual so there was no telling'.

When he shot the works an' we wound up with shakes, fries an' DOUBLE cheeseburgers, I started getting' seriously concerned. There wasn't much that could put the brakes on my appetite anyway, so I dug in an' he tried to keep up.

Chewing' an' eyeing' each other like a couple' a circling' boxers for a minute or two, he finally found an opening' somewhere between the cheeseburger an' the fries an' dove in. He talked about what a good son I was, how proud he was of how far I'd come along, an' how far I was sure to go.

Nodding' an' thanking' him between mouthfuls, I started in on the shake. He went on 'bout how "life takes you directions you hadn't always thought" an' I was 'bout convinced there was another baby coming' by then.

———

"Like for instance," he paused," the governments notion that my project would be better off in Utah."

That last bit brought me to a full stop right in the middle of a grinding' slurp. He nodded grimly while I worked my way through a full ten seconds of the dropped jaw blinking stares. Finally connecting' back up with my brain, I managed a stuttering' "S-s-say what?"

He dove in for real then an' my "fix" started coming' apart at the seams.

"Utah!" the thought stunned me again an' my eyes started dropping' slowly while he fell all over himself apologizing' an' laying' out the plusses.

There was more money, the Gran' Canyon, Disneyland', the Pacific Ocean, real live cowboys an' Indians an' all the gunfighters I'd ever heard of. "It's the original wild West son!" he finished up hopefully.

I have to admit my eyes widened a little at Disneyland. The Mickey Mouse Club was a hit with me an' the thought of meeting' Annette Funicello just about brought me around, but I still wound up looking' at my hands where they'd dropped in my lap.

"Utah..."

When we got home there was a general silence with the odd bit of crying'. It looked like mama had told the girls.

It was all I could do to blink, laying' awake pretty much all night. When the sun rose the next morning' there it was again.

"Utah?!"

The furthest I'd been away from the house was Montgomery for a basketball tournament. Utah might as well've been China for all the stories people started telling' us when they found out where we were going'.

There was one about this fellow that got captured by the Mormons. He'd only escaped by jumping' off the highest spire of their temple into the Great Salt Lake.

Rumor also had it that they'd dug tunnels under the entire United States an' would pop up every now an' then ta capture women an' make polygamist slave-wives out of 'em. Mama was about ready to keep my sisters chained up by the time we left.

Getting' ready was like a soap opera called "The Mormon Menace!". Women would show up an' help pack some dishes or some such. They'd talk like we weren't going' anywhere, or tell stories 'bout the Mormon's 'til they couldn't stand it any more. Then they'd cry a while with Mama.

A couple of weeks later we were standing' in front of an empty house with a crowd of family an' friends that had come to see us off. There was another round of tears, hand shaking', hugging', an' back slapping'. Me an' Ricky kicked at the dirt, trying' to work out exactly what was happening'. Neither one of us thought it was any good.

Grandma, mama, an' all the girls were just a mess. I just wished Grandpa could've been there, cause I just know he would've spoke kindly to daddy an' even shook his hand, knowing' he might not see us anymore.

It was right then I knew I'd miss Grandma the most. She'd been 'bout my best friend most of my life. She gave me one last "You be good Bobby" an' I promised I would through a tearful hug. The way everybody was carrying on you'd have thought we were dying instead of crowding' into the car.

Then the craziest thin' happened. That old car started moving away from all the people I'd ever known.

As we pulled away I looked back, hoping' the car would break down or daddy would stop an' tell us he was kidding', or something'...anything.

Then we'd gone too far an' they faded outta sight around a bend in the road. Roy an' Shorty crossed my mind. Turning' around an' slumping' in the seat, I realized ALL the people I'd grown up with were just memories now.

Tears were usually outta the question, but I let loose anyway then, trying' to hide my face against the window, watching' the world change as we spun along. The forest of Alabama gave way to the raised highways an' mossy trees of Louisiana. My tears dried up as people an' places I'd never seen before rolled by.

I'd spent my fair share of time wondering' what was down that road anyway. Now I'd get to find out for myself an' it wasn't a bad show really.

Before we stopped that night, we started seeing' land that looked like the western serials I'd grown up with. Every time I saw another cactus I expected Indians to jump out an' ambush the car.

We stopped that night at the first hotel I'd ever stayed in, with the first real swimming' pool I'd ever seen. Well I HAD to try that out. Getting' on my swim trunks, I took a flying' leap into the deep end.

The West had another little surprise for me then. For all those fellows I'd seen on the movie screen crawling' an' dying' in the burning' desert, begging' for a drop to drink, that water was flat COLD.

I shot back out like a shivering' blue cannon ball an' stood gawking' at that icebox of a pool. Some of daddy's words came back to me then an' straightened me up a little. "It's sink or swim son!" an' it was. My entire family was 'bout to have a whole new experience.

We were on our own now.

"Utah!"

A couple more days of that kind of traveling' an' there

we were! I'd never been around mountains like that. For the first few weeks I woke up every morning' thinking' it was going' to rain 'cause it looked overcast on the horizon.

Rain was not a very common problem in Utah though, what they called a river I wouldn't have fished in for a creek and what they called rain wasn't a drizzle where I'd been.

We got to see some snow that winter for the first time an' figured out snowballs pretty fast, but it was just plain DRY. My lips shriveled up an' the bottom one cracked right down the middle before I got educated on lip balm.

Fortunately, we were staying' with another family for a short while 'til we got on our feet. It worked out nice cause I got a little time to acclimate so I wasn't "that split lipped boy that talks funny" when we finally got moved in to our new house.

I was glad too 'cause a few days later I sat on the front porch just ta watch the world an' I tell you what it was girls night out! I guess there wasn't a teenage boy within three blocks of my house an' It wasn't too long before I was the star attraction!

My mother wasn't too worried 'bout the girls in Utah, just the men, so she made them all as welcome as she could. They'd just about line up to sit on the front porch, drink lemonade, an' take in my "foreign" accent.

School wasn't so bad either. The teachers an' students

both seemed a little nicer, though odd to me, but I'm sure that was mutual. They even had an innovation my old high school hadn't even conceived of yet. Drivers education! Son, I was ready for me an' a drivers license to be close family with all those girls around.

The first year of school went 'bout as well as you might expect with me learning' Utahan as a second language, but I hung in there. When that first report card rolled out I got some stern looks from daddy an' disappointed clucking' from mama, but they understood I was still getting my feet under me.

They felt pretty bad 'bout having to dump me out here so they gave me a little more slack, which I put to good use hanging myself with the second semester. They were none to happy about that. I didn't out an' out fail so there was no summer school, but I did wind up spending some time in my room. I'd been ordered there to consider my dwindling future prospects if I didn't straighten up some next year.

One bright spot in this was I'd finally settled on one of those neighbor girls. She was just a touch shorter than me with chestnut hair an' a smile you wouldn't believe. When she flashed that smile at me I felt lucky to be alive.

We'd walk together, go out to dances, an' the way she kissed would warm you right up. That was a good thing to cause I'd just about never seen snow before either.

Things been going pretty good for us during the school

year an' I fell for her like Niagara on the rocks! She just had to flash a smile an' bounce her pony tail an' I'd do anything she wanted. I thought that was love back then an' son I was in it!

After a month of me being grounded an' us talking over the phone I was looking forward to spending some summer with her. My first day out she'd planned up a double date an' asked me if I'd do her a favor by going with her friend 'cause she was so shy. I was NOT up for that, but she flipped her pony tail an' smiled so I fell in line.

Loading up in somebody's car that Friday night, we went to the movies. I don't even remember the movie. The girl I was with was nice, but not where I wanted to be. Especially not when I saw this fellow up front start putting the moves on her.

Before I knew what was happening, he'd kissed her! Kissed MY girlfriend!

Now if she'd said something…ANYTHING…I'd have beat him ragged, but the worst thing was she kissed him back!

I was stunned beyond reason. It felt like getting piled on back at my first football game again, an' I had the exact same reaction. I just got outta the car an' started walking. It could've been ten miles to the house. I don't remember. When I got there I just flopped down on the bed an' groaned.

Daddy looked in on me a little later. "What's the

---

problem son?" Well I have to admit I got a little surly an' gave him a "Whatta you think?" since he'd seen me leave on that date in a car an' come back on foot.

He stood there for a second pondering that when I sat up an' apologized. I told him what'd happened an' he nodded thoughtfully. "Yeah that's a pretty tough row ta hoe." he said, putting a hand on my shoulder.
Then I broke the subject that'd been on my mind since the school year ended. "Daddy, I want to go home."

He knew what I meant an' said he'd make some calls, an' he did. He figured I'd have a chance of graduating high school back there, so he got Grandma on the phone an' she was just excited 'bout the idea of having me back in our old town! I was too, for a while.

So I got on a bus an' went back the way I'd come, seeing the same sights, getting more an' more excited the closer I got. Then I was in Mobile an' Uncle Leslie was there picking me up!

He was a Fireman at the time, so his house was empty a lot. I had the run of the place for a few days an' spent a little time wondering around Mobile until the weekend, and then he drove me out to Grandma's house.

I tell you what, it was GOOD ta see Grandma. She squeezed me like nobodies business an' set us up with some cookies an' milk just like she used to an' we talked 'bout my time in Utah.

"Well!" Grandma finally said, "I expected it ta be a lot

—

worse I imagine. But I'm so glad you're here Bobby."
an' she was.

I did a lot of chores for her, putting in a garden,
chopping wood, and a fixing things that Grandpa used
ta take care of. She was pretty well set up with what
Grandpa had left an' could afford to hire somebody,
but I suppose she wanted me to feel needed an' I
appreciated it.

Well that beautiful shiny road they'd put right through
the middle of paradise had done something else I'd
never figured on…a LOT of change. I guess I hadn't
seen it while it was there 'cause it happened slow
enough, but during the year I was gone some stores
had popped up, others had come down, an' a lot of
other people had decided they needed to find out what
was up the road too. Daddy's job wasn't the only one
that had moved on or was just gone I suppose.

Ricky's family had moved away, presumably under the
influence of our fine example of upward mobility.
There were a few other friends that were still there, but
they acted like I had the mumps or something. I
suppose I spoke a little to much Utahese by now to
seem like anything other than a foreigner. As it turned
out, I pretty much didn't have any friends there an'
most other folks just seemed like they'd plain old
forgot 'bout me.

I'd traded the Willys for some other car before we left
'cause I felt sorry for this other boy. That old car had
gotten hauled off when we left anyway, so I was
walking everywhere I went an' the girls didn't care too

much for that. Safe to say any imagined improvements in my LOVE life definitely did NOT materialize. After a while of helping Grandma around the house I managed to get a job bagging groceries at a little store up the road that had managed to survive somehow. Well that fellow was apparently surviving by not paying his help, cause I worked there for a couple of months an' didn't see a flat colored penny for all the work I did.

So I left that an' went back to school, which didn't go any better than it did in Utah. I'd never been a bad student, but now I was 'bout to drown in D's an', while I'd never figured on going to Yale or even the University of Alabama, the simple assumption of a high school education began to look doubtful.

It looked like there wasn't much of a home for me there anymore. Oh I knew we'd come back an' visit an' be welcome, but me an' that town had both moved on a little too much it seemed like.

Well, I thanked Grandma, the best I could, then got on another bus back to Utah. There was a job that summer that actually paid a little. Then school started, an' it was the same old thin' again. Here I was seventeen years old an' not much better off than fifteen.

The truth of it is at that point I just plain dropped outta high school. My parents didn't take well to that at ALL an' sat me down for a serious talk. Daddy let me know it was time to do something an' Mama nodded her head an' finished half his sentences for him.

They'd never tag teamed me like that before so I knew
it was what you'd have to call double serious.
Thinking back on the little bit of life I had behind me, I
remembered a common thread. The military! I went
to sleep that night thinking 'bout it, dreamed 'bout
seeing the world, an' the next morning I could just see
myself in a sailors uniform wandering around
Singapore or loading up a big gun on a battle ship.
Yes sir, that was where I was going.

So I borrowed the car an' went ta the recruiters!

They had me take a test which I did reasonably well
on. Interviewing me made a fair impression on them
since I spoke the languages of two different states an'
had managed to expand my vocabulary a little in the
process. I knew how far up an Alabama road a "fur
piece"was an' how to "praise the lard, an' take the corn
to the horses" in Utah.

Then they stood me up to an eye chart.

Well, I don't guess I had ever complained 'bout it or
seen a doctor for it, but as it turned out I was 'bout half
an eyeball short of blind an' they turned me out like
yesterdays trash! I was in such a hurry getting out I
'bout bumped into the wall on the other side of the
hallway an' that's when I saw it!

The fellow on that poster looked 'bout as heroic as
anybody I'd ever seen. CHECK POSTER, that blue
uniform was SHARP with the epaulets an' that white
belt. Son he even had an anchor on his hat like a navy
man. I'd even heard something about marines an'

———

77

swords. I could just imagine me an' Errol Flynn getting into it over some buxom wench or some such. Son, that looked pretty good to me. So I stepped right in.

Well as it turns out, these fellows weren't as picky 'bout eyesight an' were glad to have me. It wasn't ten minutes before I'd made the first real decision of my young life, signed on the dotted line, an' shook everybody's hand! It felt pretty good at the time. Something nagged at the back of my mind though.

There was one little detail I hadn't thought about before I'd signed, but it did on the way home. There was a war on in a little place called Vietnam, an' I'd just signed up with the United States Marine Corp!

Well you can imagine how my parents reacted to that. I told 'em 'bout how I'd tried the Navy an' my bad vision an' all.

My mother just started SCREAMING! She was pacing around the house like a quarter horse, moving furniture, an' wiping at things like an electric sander.

She was going on like "No son of MINE is going to any Vietnam I didn't carry you for no NINE MONTHS to have the damned PRESIDENT get you killed, an' THEY don't KNOW who they're dealing with 'cause they're goanna UNISIGN that paper. We're going down there RIGHT NOW an' we're going to get this TAKEN CARE OF!!"

She went on like that for a solid fifteen minutes while

my dad sat there with his head in his hands. When he looked up he was grinning! I asked him what was wrong 'cause I was sure he'd lost his mind.

"Well…", he paused," The Marines wouldn't take me because of my feet."

We looked at each other for a second then started laughing'. I mean we really roared. Mama came back in the room an' started beating' both of us with that rag of hers, then declared us both insane.

Daddy grabbed her in a hug for a second an' said something I've never forgot. "Honey…", he started, but she was still winding down. "You're just CRAZY John Mizell you go GET THE CAR an' we're GOING DOWN THERE RIGHT NOW!"

"HONEY!", he finally said loudly. Well he hardly ever raised his voice an' never at Mama in my presence. She looked at him with her mouth open for a second. He just said simply, "He's goanna be all right."

Well she started crying then an' I gave her a hug myself. We both held her until she got done an' I apologized half a dozen times.

"Well," she finally said, "I guess it's done now." That was the end of that. At least I thought it was. Little did I know.

The whole family heard 'bout it at dinner an' with four sisters you can imagine there was plenty of reaction there too. I just followed Daddy's example an' kept my head down until it blew over.

A month or so later I got quite a send off at the airport. They stood there waving an' hallooing' until I couldn't see them anymore. Then I was in the air watching the clouds go by.

I felt really free for the first time in my life I guess. It didn't last long though.

BOOT

Getting off the plane, I found a taxi an' got over to the MCRD San Diego, where they loaded me, an' 'bout thirty or so other guys, on a bus. I remember the taxi driver saying "You did what!? Son don't you know there's a war on? They'll come get you when they need you anyway!"

I heard later there was a sign over the gate the bus entered through that said "Welcome to the Gates of Hell". I don't remember seeing it, but if I had later "You got that right!" would be the first words outta my mouth.

The bus stopped, an' a MAN in marine uniform stepped on, grabbed the handrail, an' eyed us for a second or so. I capitalize MAN because I know for sure if there had been any doubt as ta what a MAN could be, an' whether or not we'd seen one, they were all entirely dispelled at that point. You could see combat an' hard decisions in every line on that fellows face.

We got REAL quiet.

Then his mouth opened, boot camp BEGAN, an' my childhood officially ENDED! I don't think any of us had ever conceived the existence of a human being capable of the volume, hard driving, an' sheer abusive profanity these DI folks showed a natural talent for.

The first sentence or two shocked me straight up outta my seat like he'd stuck a cattle prod to my backside an' we spent 'bout three seconds getting off that bus any way we could. It was like the first half of a Chinese fire drill with forty guys an' one door.

That's where I met, at least if I understood his meaning correctly, my mother, my father, my new best friend, an' my worst nightmare, the man that introduced me to a whole new level of respect for authority, my Drill Instructor Corporal Easy. Now I've made up some stuff in my time but I am absolutely not kidding you, his name... was Easy.

You'll notice I capitalize Drill Instructor too, that's because if I didn't Corporal Easy would find me an' make me do fifty pushups in a foot of mud if he'd been dead for decade. Sometimes I still look around to see if he's watching when I don't get the corners right on my bed.

Corporal Easy was, by anyone's account (an' especially his own), the meanest, toughest, proudest, loudest, baldest damned black Marine you'd ever be unlucky enough to meet in a dark alley, an' some of those twice.

I tell you what, I STILL feel sorry for the first black fellow that called him "brother". I hear he turned on him like a gator on a rat. I can't recall exactly what he said but I think it was something like "I AM NOT YOUR M***** F****** BROTHER YOU N***** MAGGOT, YOU CALL ME BROTHER AGAIN AND YOU'LL FIND OUT I'M THE GOD DAMN M***** F****** BLACK SHEEP OF THE F****** ADAMS FAMILY!!!   YOU GET ME..."BROTHER"?!?!"

I'm going to say that fellow got it the first time…along with some particularly creative recreational calisthenics in a foot of mud.

I learned myself some interesting scientific principles from Corporal Easy.

Now, I'd HAD my own personal religious doubts about some aspects of evolution. Corporal Easy informed me that it was not only possible, but that it happened hourly, could work backwards in less time, an' the form of life we'd made it to depended entirely on his mood.

We were alternately worms, maggots, slime, scum, slime suckers, scum suckers, scum suckin' slime, slime suckin' maggots, an' my personal favorite...assholes. I liked that last one the best because that meant he was in a good mood.

Not only did we change species so often it would make

your head spin, but he always managed to work their mating habits an' recreational needs into just about every "conversation" just in case we were wondering where all the baby maggots came from.

Good to know.

It was also nice to finally get the goods on how to make a bed, put on underwear, put on pants, wear a hat, tie our shoes, eat our food, brush our teeth, bathe, stand up, sit down, walk, run, crap, shave, an' look at stuff.

I learned not ta look at stuff cross eyed, cause he promised that if any of us so much as gave him a cross eyed look, he'd bust our "SORRY FLAT ASSES BACK TO CLEVELAND!!!". I'd never been to Cleveland, but I was pretty sure then, an' still am now, that the devil has a summer home there if he knew Corporal Easy.

I can truthfully say if I'd known I'd been doing all that stuff wrong before I made the Corporal's acquaintance I'd have mended my ways.

Easy came in for morning inspection one sunny day an' stopped in front of me, peering closely at my face. "Did you shave Mizell!?" he demanded.

"SIR NO SIR! I was unable ta find any hair ta shave SIR!", I respectfully submitted. I was seventeen; baby faced, an' had a chin like a baby's bottom.

"DAMMIT MIZELL YOU GET YOUR ASS IN

THERE AND FIND SOME!!", he fired at me. I gave him my best "AYE AYE SIR!", immediately dug out my razor, then went an' FOUND some. I made sure ta shave twice a day after that whether I needed it or not.

A big part of everybody in my barracks wanting to get things right the first time was so Corporal Easy wouldn't feel obligated to explain it for "the TEN THOUSANDTH TIME YOU MAGGOTS!!". Not sure how I missed the first 9,999 times. I always felt cheated outta my evolution too 'cause it was always maggots just after the 9,999th time.

Come ta think of it, it seems like every time he told us something was the ten thousandth time. I'm supposing when he hit his high notes all the faces, screaming, an' swearing sort of blended every time he'd said, or heard the same thing into a single blindingly bright column of marine truth that he poured on us in molten streams of verbal abuse for "THE TEN THOUSANDTH TIME".

I tell you what, when he really got rolling those volcanic tributaries gathered into a single stunningly inspired flow that could stiffen your spine until it CRACKED. He could make your hair stand up so hard it would lift your cover right off your head.

You may think I'm kidding 'bout that, but I tell you what, it was no joke. If there was any swearing, sexual innuendo, racial slur, blasphemy, or just plain mean an' nasty thing those Drill Instructors forgot to say to us I must notta been there that day.

———

Sometimes it reminded me a little of my Grandpa's sermons. Come to think of it, my Grandpa probably could've learned a trick or two from old Easy.

We learned ta think of Corporal Easy as a higher power.

I suppose, an' I've read since, that this is all meant to break you down so they can build you back up. The problem was he wasn't strapping me like my Grandpa, slapping me daily like my teachers, beating on me like the other kids, or being any kind of mean I hadn't already gotten a double dose of.

Frankly, I mostly found it all pretty interesting if a little strenuous an' appreciated that I wasn't getting slapped around more than a reasonable dose of justice allowed.

Not that they didn't slap folks around. I heard they weren't supposed to, but they still found ways to oblige anybody that they judged to be "asking for it". You could "ask for it" by not getting things right the third time, or saying anything other than "SIR YES SIR", or "AYE AYE SIR" to anything a Drill Instructor said.

Seemed like I managed to get things right the first time more often than not though. That's something I can thank my grandfather the farmer for. He taught me not to cover the same ground twice cause it made everything take longer an' wear harder. It's Safe to say that NOBODY wanted to be under the gentle ministry of Corporal Easy longer than the absolute minimum the Marine Corp required.

Of course there's always a screw-up in most teams an' ours was no exception. We had a fellow I'll call Stanley.

Stan the man couldn't walk right, turn right, or even crap right by Easy's estimates. Easy had a long public talk with Stan on that last topic once when we'd all turned out an' he'd forgot his cover.

We started off trying hard not ta laugh an' by the end we were 'bout in tears feeling sorry for the guy. Easy was a master of abusive oration, the Cicero of profanity in my existence then an' now.

We didn't feel sorry for him much though, 'cause we were a TEAM. That meant we'd ALL failed when Stanley failed, an' failure meant "life goanna get E Z now boys" as the Corporal liked to say. Of course that's about when we went to the mud pits for "nose in" triangle pushups, alternating knee to elbow setups with ten second crunch an' holds, arm out squats with alternating ten second holds, an' whatever other twisted form of torture Richard Simmons' evil twin had consulted with Satan himself on that month.

One day, just when we thought we'd seen it all, we'd gotten our boots nice an' caked up with mud an' Stan managed to tweak Old Easy's last nerve somehow. The Corporal decided to get us on our shoulders doing air cycling in the mud with twenty pound mud caked boots just to see how long we could hold our breath.

———

Stan, of course, was the first one up so we got to go again.

Yall've heard the one 'bout the guy dropping the grenade on the throwing course. Well we had too an' were all looking for cover when Stanley stepped up to the plate.

Sure enough he pulled the pin, hauled back, an' dropped that grenade right next to Easy's boots. We all hit the dirt 'bout the same time the grenade did. Easy scooped that sucker up like he was going for donuts an' tossed it down the course while we all laid there thinking of ways ta get rid of Stan now that he'd started trying to kill us.

He was so bad we all figured he must be bucking for a discharge. As it turns out though, the marines weren't just looking for a few GOOD men in 1967. They were looking for any man that would let them slap some cameo on him and they weren't letting go for love or money once they got 'is name on the dotted line.

Stanley wound up getting hauled off to somebody's military psych ward for an "evaluation". I tell you what, those Marine psychiatrists must be something else, cause last I heard he was back in boot. They had ta have done something pretty special ta get him wanting another shot at Easy. I decided right then an' there that evaluations take place somewhere in the service tunnels under hell's basement.

I managed to get through with fairly high flying colors anyway. As a credit an' testimony to my performance

I won, by my count of Corporal Easy's, naming convention, the second most frequent asshole award. By my understanding that meant Old Easy was in a good mood, a lot when he watched me perform.

I suppose that could've been 'cause he loved putting his size 11 shiny black leather combat boot on a skinny short cracker with a southern drawl more than anything in the world, hard to say.

He did smile at me once though. Can't say for sure if it was friendly or not 'cause he had his foot on my chest during a sit-up at the time. Still, I don't remember him smiling at anybody else.

Maybe I only remember all the good times.

About the end of basic he called me into 'is office. He had a stack of papers in front of him he was filling out. "Mizell," he started, "I need to know what you want ta be buried under."

Naturally I was thinking dirt an' a stone would probably do like for most people so I asked, "Sir?"

"Buried under, you know, religion.", he insisted seriously.

"You mean like Baptist?"

"Yeah, baptized."

"No, I mean, Baptist."

———

"Yeah that's right."

"Sir?"

"Baptized, yeah, what church were you baptized into."

"Baptist sir."

"I said that already son, you're about to get on my nerves."

"Sir?"

"Dammit Mizell, I haven't got time for this!", he looked at my papers again, "Ok then, says here you're from Utah, so YOU'RE MORMON, now GET THE HELL OUTTA HERE!!!"

My head was spinning by then, but I automatically saluted an' left, wondering what had just happened. Near as I can tell, my Southern Alabama drawl had got in the way there. It wasn't the end of it though.

That very next day a couple of Mormon Missionaries showed up talking 'bout me being a Mormon. I figured it had something to do with Corporal Easy so I was as polite as I could be. The next thing I knew they'd got me in the water an' I WAS one. It all happened so fast, like everything in basic. You just went with everything that seemed official.

I decided right then an' there that some things that happen in boot camp STAYED in boot camp. I never told anybody 'bout it. It wasn't just that Mormons weren't real popular back then either. You've got to remember my Grandpa had been a Holy Roller with a MEAN temper, an' my mama simmered 'bout two degrees shy of blowing her top on a GOOD day. I'd have just about been HUNG if I ever got back to a family reunion with THAT little piece of history tagging along.

There was no way on Gods green earth I was going to go home an' tell them that the United States Marine Corp had made a MORMON outta me!

Well…anyway, the good news was we all got a month's leave after basic an' I went back to Utah to visit my family before infantry training. It was uneventful but nice. We all knew the possible consequences of what I was doing so there was a tearful goodbye at the airport with my whole family.

It felt a little like a funeral, but I guess we ALL had to deal with that possibility. This was the last time they'd see me until I got my first leave after shipping out. We said our last goodbyes an' I boarded the plane, waving an' smiling at all of them as I climbed up the boarding ramp.

Two weeks back from leave, doing well in Infantry training, one day I walked into the CO's office ta pick up my mail where I'd been told there was a letter for me. Walking in I could tell something was up because the Gunny was personally holding the already open letter and giving me a stern look. Turned out some of the other guys had opened the letter for a joke 'cause they saw it was from a girl, an' it was. The Gunny

---

quietly handed the letter to me, looking at me
expectantly, so I started reading.

It was a letter from my sister Nancy saying she was
PREGNANT! It was good news an' I was pleased ta be
an Uncle, but was pretty pissed off 'bout the letter
being opened. Figuring I better not say anything about
it, I clamped my mouth shut an' looked at the Gunny.
When he saw I had no comment he told me we had to
go in an' see the MAJOR.

Naturally I was thinking to myself "What the hell is the
big deal 'bout a letter from my sister?!". I was furious
by the time we made it to the Majors office so it was a
downright galling an' HERCULEAN effort keeping
my mouth shut by now. They'd opened my mail an'
they were taking ME to the Majors office?!

Saluting, I stood there stonily silent at full attention
while the Gunny explained to the major that the letter
indicated I'd gotten my girlfriend pregnant.

My anger all turned to disgust an' disbelief in a split
second. All I could do was stand there shocked with
my mouth open, staring at the Gunny. The Major took
the letter an' gave it a cursory glance. I guess he took
my shocked look for a confession 'cause then he said,
"Well son, for the good of the service you're going to
have to go home and marry this girl."

My head felt like it spun completely around as I threw
an even MORE stunned look at the Major. He was
nonplussed an' continued like he was asking for a cup
of coffee, "We're giving you another thirty days leave

to get the job done and that's an order."

I was past speechless at this point, but another thirty days leave sounded pretty good to me. Sounded like pretty good payback for opening my mail too. All I could do was shake my head an' blink. Finally snapping back to full attention an' giving an enthusiastic "Aye Aye SIR!", I did a crisp ninety degree turn an' marched out the door.

My SQUAD thought I'd lost my mind when I got there 'cause I must' a laughed my head off for 'bout the whole time I was packing . The stewardesses on the flight home kept an eye on me too, since I couldn't help occasionally giggling for no apparent reason.

My whole family was shocked to see me again an' got a big kick outta my "orders". True to my command I did ask my sister ta marry me right at a family dinner with her husband sitting there about busting a gut laughing . She said she appreciated my generous offer, but declined due to the legal complication of bigamy, an' added that she didn't find me very attractive anyway.

Spending the next thirty days doing my best to fulfill the spirit of the Majors order, I dated as many of the girls, in my neighborhood, as possible, in hopes of finding , some marriage material. Not much luck there, but I did have a wonderful time!

The day before my flight back ta California, Dad woke me up at five AM before he went to work. He knew I wanted to use their 57 Chevy sedan, but needed a ride

—

an' asked if I'd drive. Seemed like a good idea, so I threw some clothes on an' we had breakfast together then left.

Base security waved us through an' I dropped off dad an' started back home for a little more sleep. The light wasn't working, so I gave a careful look up and down the road, and then started across. Guess I was groggier than I thought because 'bout the time I got into the intersection of the highway, a flash of color caught the corner of my eye.

My head seemed to turn in slow motion. Makin' out the shiny grill work of the car, my eyes tracked up to the drivers shocked face just before that beautiful chrome hood ornament seemed to smash almost directly into my left shoulder. A car that I later found out was going 'bout seventy miles an hour T-BONED me.

I wasn't wearing a seat belt an' I recall bouncing around the inside pretty good. Getting out the passenger side, I ran over to the other car. The driver had smashed his face on the steering wheel and was bleeding pretty good. People had stopped, so I yelled for somebody to call an ambulance.

The driver moaned, lifting his head off the steering wheel. Blood spurted out all over the place so I tore off my shirt, wadding it up to press to 'is forehead.

He knew his name when I asked, which it was a relief to me. Being taught a little first aid in basic, I made sure to keep him conscious until the ambulance arrived in case of a concussion. We talked 'bout his family for a few minutes an' he asked me to call them. I promised I would an' took the number.

It was a big relief when sirens blared in the distance an' came closer until finally the ambulance rolled up. The attendants pulled the driver out onto a fold-up gurney an' applied a proper dressing to 'is head.

One of them looked at my car an' whistled. "This guys goanna be fine," he said, "but I wouldn't give a dime for that other guy. Where's he at?"

I told him it was me an' he looked shocked an' immediately made me lie down on the ground. He looked me over once an' said I was lying. I repeated it was me an' they asked the other driver, who glanced over at me an' said, "Yeah that's him."

"That's impossible!", the attendant said, shaking his head ,"There's not a bruise on you!" I hadn't even thought of it up 'til then but he was right.

Looking back at the Chevy now, I could see the door an' the side post had been pushed in at least a couple of feet an' the whole frame was bent. It didn't make sense, but here I was.

Mama was just glad I was alright an' thanked God for it while she checked me up an' down, apparently to make sure nothing was missing. Daddy took it surprisingly well that night when I came by in a borrowed car ta pick him up an' explained what'd happened.

I hadn't said any bedtime prayers in a long time but that night I had a pretty good talk with God an' realized why my dad was ok with what'd happened. He an' I both thought it was a sign, an' hoped it was a GOOD one. His words came back to me then..."He's goanna be all right." I was about ready to believe it myself now.

We had to borrow another car to take me to the airport the next morning. Mama didn't want to go, saying "I've been through that once an' it's ENOUGH!", so my dad an' I drove alone.

We talked a surprising amount about surprisingly little. It was like we just wanted to hear each other's voice an' were trying to work around to something else, but couldn't admit it an' couldn't quite get to it.

Looking back as I boarded the flight to California, dad stood almost at attention, looking steadily at me as though he were taking a picture. There was a single tear on 'is face. Beginning to tear up myself, I waved one last time, an' ducked into the plane.

Sadly I had ta report back to the Major that I had asked the girl but she'd turned me down an' said I was an UGLY sumbitch to boot. He excused me then handed me orders to report to infantry training.

It was a nice change from the abuse of basic. We'd run twenty miles a day when we weren't hiking to bivouac locations for training. One camp during a particularly bad storm, I got caught in a flood wrapped up in my

—

sleeping bag an' had to hold on for dear life to a couple of trees as the torrent tried to wash me down the hill side.

We did advanced weapon training with mortars, M79 launchers, an' M72 LAW rockets. That last one was a lotta fun.

Things went well enough there that I made Corporal. Then somebody put out a request for corporals to apply for Vietnamese language training an' I JUMPED on it! Honestly, I was ready to apply every brain cell available (not that I lay claim to any great excess of those) to ANYTHING that would keep me from shipping out! Turned out I was a pretty fair hand with the language too. Most of the fellows in the Marines that I knew felt the same way about shipping out to Vietnam.

Learning Vietnamese earned me another stripe an' they sent me to advanced infantry training. I tell you what, I started feeling like a by God Marine SERGEANT by then.

Eight men would be counting on me to bring them back alive. Lieutenants would be counting on me to get the job done. I was going to by God, Semper Fidelis, 'damn the torpedoes get it done no matter how many unfortunate bastards I had to introduce to the business end of the fairly wide variety of destructive devices an' tactics I was fluent with by this time.

They'd assigned me to the squad I'd be shipping out with in a month by then, an' they seemed like some pretty rough old boys. A couple seemed more like they should be in prison than the Marines even. It was a mixed squad of white an' black fellows, but they were all ready to roll as far as I could tell.

We drilled, fought, ran, an' bunked together for a month an' felt like we were a pretty competent fire team by the time the orders came on a Thursday. We were shippin' out ta Vietnam in FOUR DAYS!

That night, our squad got together an' took up a collection for one fellow to fly home that weekend. We put all our names in a hat an' 'bout the roughest white boy in that bunch pulled one out. It was mine!

Figuring they'd all be mad at me, I told them to draw again since I'd already had sixty days. They all just smiled an' some of them shook their heads. "No sir," he grinned, dumping the hat into the garbage, "You just one lucky damn marine." "I reckon so." I said, trying my best to be gracious about it, "Guess I'll go then."

Too young an' naive at the time, I realized much later they'd probably WANTED me outta the way so they could have some REAL fun, an' MY name was probably the only one in that HAT. They all had unspent pay an' probably figured ten bucks apiece ta have their Sergeant off their back last weekend before Vietnam was pretty near damn well worth it.

I didn't even call my family, just popping up at the front door that night. They were a little confused, but VERY glad ta see me!

We talked 'bout all my training an' I spoke some Vietnamese for them. They were astonished that any child they produced could speak anything REMOTELY like Chinese an' kept making me say things like "Where's the bathroom?" an' "This is United States government property, leave immediately!" until I begged for mercy.

Mama made the best meal I'd ever seen for lunch the day I was leaving an' I mean it was a FEAST! We all ate, talked, an' laughed until it was time to go.

That was one of the best times I ever had with my family an' I was glad I'd gone. The goodbyes had been said three times now, so this time it was just a taxicab an' some waving from the front porch as I rolled outta sight to the airport on a Sunday afternoon.

California was a blur of preparation that Monday. Reunited with my squad, there was a LOT to do. Signing', shufflin', preppin', packing, inspection, an' being inspected, until finally we were carrying our bags up the gangplank to the troop ship AP-110 General John Pope.

The John Pope, was a WWII troop carrier, and was the very ship an Uncle of mine, had gone to the South Pacific, on in 1945. His war consisted of arriving' on Iwo Jima after it'd been taken, then bein' shipped home some months later, after the Japanese had surrendered. I couldn't help, but HOPE I'd have the same luck.

—

Daddy, hadn't had that kind of luck. He'd shipped out, early in the war, pilotin' a landin' craft on the troop ship Alhena, during the Marine assault on Guadalcanal. He was at sea, when the Japanese submarine I-4, put a torpedo into the hold, that just about killed him ,an' that was IT for him.

Being pretty much still a kid, and a Marine Sergeant, I wanted the top bunk and got it. Poor judgment on my part since the racks were seven high, that tub tossed like a cork, and I pretty much puked my way all 9,000 miles to the South China Sea off the coast of Vietnam.

New to the Navy and groggy from puking, I wondered barefoot into the head and propped myself on a urinal ta piss. Feeling a little better and looking around, there was a PFC with a toothbrush in his open mouth staring at me on my left and a corporal washing 'is hands and grinning on my right. Looking down, I realized that tiny stainless steel "urinal" had water taps.

I stood up straight, zipped with more conviction than I felt, said "As you were!", and padded back to my bunk.

More or less recovered by the time we arrived, the order came to disembark.

Getting' my still queasy self and eight marines squared away and up onto the deck, we were greeted by a frenzy of shouted orders, confused green marines, angry officers, and the bouncing' ocean all working together to provide us with an interesting morning'. It

---

was quite a scene.

Landing craft were circling' the ship and a Chaplain stood on a raised cargo hatch saying a loud prayer for the safety of the troops. The nets were dropped, and we were ordered over the side.

That's when I saw my first Marine die.

Our Corporal David Hull preceded me over the rail. He was 5'2" tall and his pack was half 'is weight, but he was a Marine. When the order came, he threw himself over the rail like he'd been doing it all 'is life.

I saw his face for a second over the gun whale. His eyes opened wide, his mouth worked noiselessly, and he clawed at the air as he fell over backwards. He got a piece' a the edge' a the net but it wasn't enough.

Rushing the rail, we saw him hit the water in the narrow gap between the boats, breathing a collective sigh of relief when he began yelling and clawing at 'is pack. Marines were rushing to pull him out, and had almost reached him when a small breaking wave shoved the 15 tons of the LCA up against the 12,000 tons of the John Pope.

When we could see him again, he wasn't struggling anymore.

Too shocked to move, we stared at the floating body as they fished it out. "Over the side boys.", came a quiet voice from behind us. I turned to see a bird Colonel who had to have seen what happened.

"Sir.." I started, blinking, my mouth moved without finding the right words. "Over the side.", he repeated quietly, but firmly. A muted chorus of "Aye Aye Sir." responded, and we went over the rail.

They had a rope on the body, and began hauling him up as we descended. I couldn't help looking into the face that had smiled at me only a few minutes ago. He spun slowly, dangling limp on the rope as he rose through the air past us. We slowed to watch. Water drained from his mouth and nose, and there was a blank, almost alive, stare on his face. It was a look I'd actually seen when he was thinking about home. We could hear the calls for a body bag up on deck.

"I said MOVE!!", the Colonel on deck was roaring at us now. "AYE AYE SIR!" came a little more loudly and we quickly dropped into the LCA.

The landing craft was probably the same type Daddy piloted. I realized now that he'd dumped boatloads of boy's just like me onto the sand and water of Guadalcanal.

I'd heard driving these LCAs was a tough job, I realized why now. They'd churn in again and again, driving in until the water was red and marines floated like so many camouflage channel markers, until it was all they could do to drop the gate and let them die. It might have been easier to die.

In that moment it occurred to me that we might be the best, but we weren't the only ones good at killing

...definitely not then an' prob'ly not now.

That death affected every marine on the ship. It was quiet and tense in our boat and I'm sure others. We were all probably thinking the same things. Running into God knows what when that door dropped and hoping if it came to it that we'd get to die a little more heroically than Corporal Hull.

My hands began to hurt and I looked down. My knuckles were white. Taking a deep breath, my grip loosened, and I waited for the gate to drop.

The bottom of the craft grounded, the signal came, and that giant slab of metal pitched open. We rushed forward a dozen steps and threw ourselves on the ground just like they'd trained us, scanning for muzzle flashes to concentrate our fire on.

Bright lights and clicking noises of cameras exploded around us. It took a moment to realize that the only resistance we'd face was the crowd of photographers eager to take advantage of our FEAR for a good COVER SHOT!

We stood up sheepishly, and in front of us on the sand was the biggest, fattest, baldest Marine Master Sergeant I'd EVER seen. He seemed a little surprised at what he must have taken for enthusiasm. "Well now that's what I like to see!", he hollered at us around the stub of a cigar, "Welcome to Vietnam marines...FALL IN!" We marched off to some transports and were hauled to camp.

My first real taste of the Vietnam I remember was on the way back to a ship on assignment to sort out a vehicle. A small sun burnt Vietnamese man wearing pieces of American uniform and a long knife was by the landing zone anxiously accosting everybody that got near with a string of mushrooms of some kind. I figured maybe they were the magic kind until I walked by and he rushed up to sell me a souvenir.

They were human ears.

Some seemed delicate and small, maybe from women or children. Ears screaming at me all at once that this was like no place I'd ever been.

Recoiling from this apparently soulless monster, I pulled my pistol on him and dressed him down in my best broken Vietnamese, channeling my Drill Instructor directly into his face. My lack of expertise in colloquial expletives notwithstanding, there's no doubt my disapproval registered.

Other marines, hearing the commotion, gathered around to back me up and he exercised the better part of whatever apparently dubious version of valor he understood. The most surprising thing, though, was that he seemed surprised. One man with a knife generally knows to walk away from a crowd of riled up marines carrying automatic weapons anyway, and he left in an odd huff.

The next thing I knew I was in some Navy Commander's office and by God if he didn't sound like he'd trained my DI! He let me know that our valued allies were not to be treated like anything other than fellow marines, and that he would personally stick my redneck ass in a can and kick it all the way to Kentucky if he ever had to deal with me again!

If there's anything a West coast marine is good at it's "AYE AYE SIR!" and "SIR YES SIR!" I gave him my best salvo of both until he got tired of asking me if I understood. By the time he got done with me I was pretty sure I'd rather kiss that ear rattling bastard on BOTH cheeks rather than talk to that Commander again.

Now THERE was a man that knew his way around the DEEP dark end of the English language and wasn't shy about sharing his TALENT. If Easy had been my first real professor of the high art of chewing expletives, I'd just done my thesis. My education in that area felt complete, and my ass felt about half chewed off. I even thought about checking on the way back to my squad just to make sure none was missing.

Deciding to walk around the camp a little to clear my head, I found myself near a razor wire vehicle compound with some Marine guards at the gate. Walking by, I was suddenly in the company of a fellow who seemed to KNOW me. He touched my arm, then jabbered in what I thought was Korean, nodding his head at me.

Apologizing for my ignorance, I stopped to listen to him for a moment, supposing if I stared at him long enough I'd magically understand what he was saying I guess. He reached into a bag and pulled out a tiger striped ARVN uniform, pointing at it and then back at something inside that compound.

He kept pushing the uniform at me and started raising his voice, so I nodded at him and took the uniform, trying to be polite. The conversation ended abruptly as he bowed and went off toward the gate of that compound.

Well…I started after him a few steps; just SURE he was going to get a real beating from those big old boys guarding that gate. He walked right past the marine guards like they weren't even THERE, started up a brand new US Army issue OD colored tow truck, and just DROVE off, waving and smiling at me as he went by.

Looking down at the uniform in my hands, then back up at the dangling bouncing hook on the quickly receding wrecker, I decided that Vietnam was a strange place.

We got a new Corporal that seemed all right. He'd been here for a few months and requested my permission to tie up some personal loose ends. I wasn't sure how I felt about anybody replacing Hull yet so I told him go ahead.

So I settled in, inspected my men, washed my underwear, kept my head down, and prayed somebody else would get on that Commander's b-list before I managed to screw up again or ship out.

I'd just got through rinsing some laundry when a siren wound up. We stood and craned our necks at the ominous sound to see what we could.

In retrospect, a camp closer to the established troop area would've been a good idea. The "cherry" Marines there got the benefit of seeing established camps scrambling for cover and heard the cries of "INCOMING!" that only swept like a wave toward us on the far edge where I stood almost stupidly as the first rockets hit.

The small mushroom clouds were surreal until the shockwaves started hammering us. The ground and any hole we could find immediately became our new best friend as DOZENS of two hundred pound North Vietnamese rocket warheads just SHREDDED that camp wherever they landed. Shrapnel tore through tents, cargo, and Marines.

My FIRST emotion was ANGER!

They were trying to kill my men! Hell, they were trying to kill me! I felt stupid, angry, helpless, and scared all at the same time as debris and MORE rockets rained on us and I couldn't even shoot BACK!

All my training and patriotism seemed set to disintegrate in a puff of grey smoke. The only sign I'd made it to Vietnam would be two smoking boots and the shocked looks and bleeding ears of my squad. I was ready to stuff MYSELF in a howitzer if it was aimed at those bastards.

Dust, gravel, and shrapnel, scattered and settled as the attack ended and the all clear sounded. I checked my men, ears ringing, yelling their names. We'd all survived our first attack, no thanks to me.

There hadn't been any direct hits on our section and not enough damage to warrant any assistance requests to us, so we just went about our business and tried to get some sleep that night to the tune of MORE rockets around midnight. I'd hoped to hell I'd get to sleep on something that didn't move that night, but I guess it was just too much to wish for. The rockets started coming in and the machine guns and artillery were firing back. It was a MESS.

Looking around I actually saw some fellows sleeping right through it. Good Lord! I was for sure they didn't have the sense God gave a GOAT! It could've been me few months later though.

When I rolled out the next morning it was raining. You may have heard it before, but I'll say it again, if there was anything I eventually figured out Vietnam knew how to do, it was ROCKETS and RAIN.

I did eventually stop being surprised at how often mornings in Vietnam started with both. This was the first of many wet days to come and not even the beginning of rocket barrages.

I'd gotten the word that we were being moved North to man a post near Dong Ha that day. I think it was a firebase, but I don't remember.

We'd got all our gear squared away and were huddled together smoking and talking when a truck pulled up. A towheaded fellow with glasses shoved his head out the window and yelled "Mizell? You with First Marine?"

"Sure enough! You our ride?" I asked. "Yes sir!" He threw a half hearted salute out the window, "I'm here to take you North. You ready to roll?"
"Ready as I'll ever be." I confirmed.

He whistled, looking around as I got my squad loaded up, "Well I'd heard you had some fireworks, but I hadn't seen it yet." "More or less." I had to agree. "Well", he continued, "you better get used to it, they get close enough for mortars to where you're going." I wasn't sure if he expected me to thank him for that information or not.

"Say!" he continued, "You want to ride up front?" "No sir!" I declined as I swung my pack on and started to the back, "I'll ride with my men." "Suit yourself, it's goanna get a little nasty back there though." I had to look at him then, "You getting a little lonely up there Corporal?" He stared at me with his mouth open for a second, and then laughed out loud as he started grinding the six by into gear. Hurriedly throwing my bag in the back and pulling myself over the gate, the truck started moving.

We bumped along quietly for a while, each collecting his own thoughts about what lay ahead, and what we'd left behind. We'd felt each other out during training and on the John Pope where there wasn't anything else to do, and seemed to fit well enough.

Some of those boys seemed like they ought to be in JAIL to me, like I said, but they all were ready to pull a trigger. I knew I'd put it on the line for them and felt like they'd do the same for me.

It was good team. I knew I'd seen AND heard of worse and felt lucky to have some of these boys with me. Frankly I would have been SCARED if I'd known some of the rest were on the other side.

After a while one of the Privates started up with something like, "Say Sergeant, you figure they got some booze at this place?" he smiled. "Now how on Gods green Earth would I know that." I grinned back, shaking my head. "Well I'm just sayin', thasall." He finished, becoming suddenly quiet.

Then another started up, "Yeah booze." and about half of them nodded in agreement. There was quiet again for a moment, "So how 'bout some weed?" another started up and a couple more nodded their heads.

The sudden starts and stops in conversation seemed odd, and I chalked it up to jitters at first. I mean after all I'd been sick all the way here and then hadn't slept since I'd arrived.

It continued like that. They connected and talked with each other in a way that just seemed wrong. I'm not sure how to explain it. It was like they were in some kind of a club that I didn't have the handshake for. Sharing a secret that I couldn't know.

Starting to feel a little worn by it, I started wondering if maybe I should've rode up front after all. It continued like that for a while. Fits of conversation, like they were trying to gnaw through to something none of us could put our finger on.

Finally I'd had enough, maybe because I was still a little off from the ocean crossing. "Pipe the HELL down for a while!" I snapped and immediately regretted it. "Just trying to lighten it up a little Serge." Our new Corporal said, trying to blunt my impact a little, grinning at me a little too broadly. They were all staring at me now.

Their eyes didn't even seem to blink right as they glanced at each other then back at me. I wanted to be out of the back of that truck in the worst way right then, wishing again I'd taken the driver up on his offer, anywhere but the back of that truck where things were just wrong.

Then, as plain as day, it felt like a sort of tunnel opened up into my mind. I heard a small quiet voice plainly say…

"Jump."

It startled me so much...I DID.

Jumping out of the back of the six by at about twenty miles an hour as it slowed for a turn, my rifle tore out of my hand and bounced behind me as I rolled about ten feet and came to rest on my side. Watching the truck turn to go over a bridge, I made out the face of the white Private who'd drawn my name. He rose to his feet and stared at me with his mouth open. I thought of his words..."You just one lucky damn Marine".

He disappeared in a geyser of dirt and fire a split second before the shockwave pushed and bounced me back along the road. Pieces of bridge, earth, and I'm sure my squad, rained down all around me.

I found out later that the NVA would find unexploded bombs from our raids and use them. Some Viet Cong Sappers had put one of our own 500 pound bombs right under the main timbers of that bridge.

Laying there shocked for what felt like an eternity, I leapt to my feet and sprinted over to do what I could for them. Getting nearer to the flaming wreck, I slowed and swung my rifle around at an imagined enemy presence, expecting mortars or small arms fire any second.

The blast had picked up the front of the truck and turned it sideways so I reached the driver first. There was blood all over the inside of the cab like a giant hand had grabbed him and SQUEEZED.

His head was against what was left of the window and I couldn't make out the details of his face through the waterfall of blood still pouring down the glass. He'd put his palm against the glass and I instinctively put my hand against the other side and held it there.

111

His hand slid away and he was clearly dead, the first man I'd ever seen killed by Charlie. I stood staring with my hand stuck to that glass until a moan from the back tore me away from what I'd have to say was my first real communion with death.

Running around to the back, I almost threw up when I saw what was left of my squad. One of the ones nearest the gate stirred so I yanked it open and pulled him out. It was our new replacement Corporal. No one else moved.

Laying him on the ground, his eyes stared a question at me that never got answered. He started mouthing some words, asking for his mother I think, delirious with pain and trying to hold in something where his stomach had been.

 I pulled my poncho off and laid it over him to keep the rain off at least, promising...hoping, that help would be there soon. We were still so close to town, they HAD to have heard that and be sending a chopper to check it out.

I stood up over him with my M-16 in my hands just in time to see a small group of Vietnamese farmers running toward us. "STOP!" I yelled at them in English, forgetting I knew Vietnamese in the shocked daze of what I'd just witnessed. "Get back or I'll SHOOT!" I didn't have any idea what the enemy looked like yet and all I saw was a swarm of gooks with hidden knives.

They kept coming, I'm sure now to help, but they were lucky I didn't unload on them and create a SECOND tragedy. "STOP!" I screamed in Vietnamese this time. It rang hollowly in my head. Trying to fire some warning shots, I could only make puffs of smoke come out the end of my gun. For some reason they all jumped and ran off anyway with shocked backward glances. I realized then that the explosion had deafened me.

In what seemed like a few minutes there was a heavy thumping vibration and I was NEVER so glad to see ANYTHING as I was that chopper circling, probably getting a read on the situation. Waving them in frantically, I ran almost under the skids before they'd even hit the GROUND, filling them in and begging for medivac for that Corporal to the hospital.

One of the corpsmen checked the truck and verified the others were all dead while a couple of others got the Corporal loaded up. As they lifted off a jeep rolled up with a couple of boys from CID in it.

They treated the incident like a traffic ticket. My ears rang as they asked me inane questions about details that could only matter to someone who didn't realize what had just happened to my squad. How fast were we going, where we were heading.

Then they asked me why I was still alive.

Not really knowing, I paused to collect my thoughts, but, "I don't know. I guess I went out of the gate.", was all I could think of and all I could say. I don't remember answering any more questions after that. One of them came back from a radio conversation at the jeep, looking grim. "Sorry Sergeant, your Corporal didn't make it." I put my head in my hands and the world started to spin.

"You all right Sergeant?", one of them asked. Nodding at the ground, looking around for something familiar, I asked, "Where do I go now?" They looked at each other for a second, "We'll give you a ride back to CID and your division can pick you up from there." I nodded again, still dazed, ears ringing, and started toward their jeep.

Next thing I new I was sitting in a CID headquarters building, waiting for something, not sure what. I'd gotten my ass kicked to hell and back in two days and didn't feel like much of a Marine anymore, that was for damn sure. There wasn't enough spit or vinegar left in me to fill a thimble.

Nobody came from 1st Marine that evening and I spent a fitful night in the CID waiting room, afraid to sleep because I kept seeing their faces.

The Sergeant that came from 1st marine division headquarters to pick me up around noon the next day must have heard what happened 'cause he went out of his way to let me be during the drive. It was all different when we got back to division headquarters. The CID had their go at me and they wanted theirs too.

I wasn't sure what to tell them. Images of what I'd seen in the back of that truck kept running through my mind. My memories of who they'd been juxtaposed on what they'd become a split second later. The investigators were saying something but it wasn't making sense.

My squad was staring at me again, accusing me of something. The truck spun in circles as it turned over that bridge. I was flying through the air repeatedly now, slamming into the ground like a jackhammer while that final stare bore into my soul.

They asked for "observations of indigenous persons at the scene" or something like that and I looked up at the Lieutenant sitting across from me.

"You just one lucky damn marine." he choked. Broken ribs stuck out through his uniform and I could see bone and cartilage through the shredded skin on the left side of his face.

I threw up on the table and the interview broke up at that point. "Get this man a rack." he ordered, wiping at his shirt.

It was a few days more before I wanted anything to eat. I slept mostly and the dreams weren't good even though they seemed to help. The third day I woke up hungry as a bear and ready to kill and eat one myself. The mess food tasted like a home cooked FEAST.

QUESTION: Where was marine first division headquarters relative to Tien shaw?

I suppose I was better, how much I wasn't sure, but I

115

was awake and eating. The Lieutenant came by and ordered me to report to Camp Tien Shaw for assignment. Guess they thought I was good enough.

A private showed up to drive me over. As the jeep spun through the streets I saw a group of ARVN regulars that had some other Vietnamese tied up facing a brick wall. They started shooting them in the back of the head as we drove by. Three of them were dead by the time we passed. I guess they were VC, it was hard to tell. It was almost always hard to tell.

Looked to me like Vietnam wasn't just a strange place, life was pretty CHEAP here too.

TIEN SHAW

When I arrived at Tien Shaw, they assigned my quarters, gave me a meal voucher for the chow hall, and left me alone for a few days.

Tien Shaw was about as regular as life got in Vietnam. There was a mess hall, and a decent place to sleep. I had the same nightmares pretty much every night, but there didn't seem to be much I could do about it. There were rockets about every night still, but for whatever reason I could sleep some now.

That's when I met Captain Cong.

I was ordered to report to the Gunny so I rolled out and marched over. He was there with a Vietnamese Officer. Handing me orders to report to White

---

Elephant, he introduced me to the my new commanding officer, Captain Cong.

That was kind of a surprise since White Elephant was one of the three main war planning centers in Vietnam, I didn't see myself as the office type, and I'd never expected to take orders from any South Vietnamese. Orders are orders though, so I saluted and just like THAT I was working for the South Vietnamese.

My official orders were "miscellaneous duties" and I still slept at Tien Shaw, but my actual duty posting was the ARVN Transportation Command at White Elephant under the command of Captain Cong. I was now the Marine Liaison to that unit. Nice title, but my "miscellaneous duties" consisted of just doing whatever he told me to do, and all my liaisoning was after hours.

A pretty big chunk of "miscellaneous duties" was a lot of errand boy stuff. It turns out that any war would grind to a screeching halt if enough trees aren't cut down and turned into requisition and report forms. A big part of my job at first was making sure those got wherever I was ordered to get them to, and getting them signed by whoever was important enough to sign.

Mostly that meant riding around in jeeps and helicopters, and pretty much staying out of the regular shooting war. There were the usual rocket and mortar attacks, snipers, and the odd VC sabotage, but there was no getting away from that stuff anyway.

The paper work I delivered was mostly pretty standard stuff. There was ONE however, that led to more trouble than I could admit to wanting. One day the Captain handed me a standard looking attaché case that felt a little heavier than what I was used too and ordered me to get on a chopper and deliver the case to some tribal leader up in the hills.

When we touched down the pilot kept the rotors spinning and as soon as I jumped out I could tell why. I was IMMEDIATELY in the presence of a lot of VERY rough looking, suspicious, and heavily armed Vietnamese men!

Now this wasn't entirely unexpected. There WAS a war on after all, and everybody had guns and everybody was pointing them at everybody else. This situation still seemed unusual for some reason.

Asking where their officer was they nodded toward who I wanted without moving their gun barrels or taking their eyes off me. It was suddenly VERY nice to hear those rotors spinning behind me.

Walking into the building in question, there were instantly a number of automatic weapons pointed at me. Stating my business, the barrels lowered just a bit and I was nodded into an inner room where a whip like fellow admitted to being who I was looking for.

Grabbing the case out of my hands, he scrabbled greedily at the latches, but it was locked. When he insisted on having the key I hesitantly informed him I hadn't been given one. Pulling out a bush knife, he sliced it open, spilling the contents on the table.

I tell you what, that was the MOST money I'd EVER seen before or since! There must have been over a hundred thousand dollars in that stack! A thin smile came and went from his face in a split second. "You go now." he as much ordered as requested without even bothering to LOOK at me.

I'd rarely been more pleased to leave anywhere in my life. Yelling at the pilot to go before I even hit the hatch, the chopper jumped into the air, slamming me into my seat.

"You have any idea who these folks are?", I yelled over the rotors. "Not a clue!", he insisted, "I didn't like it though!" I had to smile at that, here was a fellow with the right kind of hair on the back of his neck. If I could, I was goanna fly with him next time too.

About a week later, I and one of the other aides were walking down a side street in Da Nang when a truck pulled up next to us. Next thing I knew my boots were off the ground and there was a BAG over my head. Not that I remember much here, but I'm pretty sure a sudden attack of bludgeonitis led directly to me waking up in a warehouse tied up by my thumbs, my feet swinging in the air.

The bag came off and I was looking at some people I didn't know and whose acquaintance I'd have been glad to defer. They sure seemed familiar with me though. They wore plain OD uniforms with no markings at all. One of them smoked while a blunt nosed, ham fisted white fellow worked me up and down some. A skinny black guy coached him and held me like a heavy bag, offering encouragement. "That was pretty good man, work the face some!", like that.

They had the other aide tied up in a chair with a nice view of the action. He'd let out an intermittent "Oh God!" and other sympathetic exclamations when they got a particularly nice red spray out of me, partly because he was so close it was landing on him. Come to think of it, they probably sat him there on purpose. As soon as I got a break to breath and spit some blood, I made a point of asking what they wanted.

The smoking man finally spoke up and said he thought that was a good question. I'm supposing he was the brains of the outfit. Stepping over to where I hung, he looked down his nose at me and held up something. Focusing on what he'd picked up for a second I saw the title "Louisville Slugger".

Now I love America's favorite pass time, and even played third base on our church team, but about the LAST thing I wanted to see in THIS fellows hands was a high quality baseball bat. "I'm thinking you were looking at a lot of money recently." he quietly insisted.

My eyes must have widened a little and gave me away when he said that 'cause he immediately whacked me in the stomach with that bat when I didn't answer quick enough. He said he was asking as nice as he could and suggested I speak up some in case his buddy felt like asking me some more. "He's not so good with words" he lamented, "like me." That trained ape of his grinned broadly and rubbed his knuckles.

He prodded me with the bat and started me swinging by my thumbs, which hurt like hell, then tapped me lightly a few times on the back of the skull as he walked around me.
"There's just no telling what might happen to somebody that doesn't know how to share.", he warned. My back exploded in pain as he stopped my swinging completely with a blow from the bat. Grabbing my ear, he pulled my head close to his mouth. "Bad things.", he suggested. The black fellow cackled loudly.

At that point I was pretty sure he was serious, but for some reason I just couldn't bring myself to tell him anything. Not that I'm particularly heroic, just I'd been beat PLENTY in my life by a LOT of people for a LOT of reasons. This being the first time for big money and all, I wasn't going to give him more satisfaction than I had anybody ELSE.

Even if I told him the truth I was pretty sure it wasn't going to help much anyway. I really didn't know anything and saying so would've just made things worse.

Holding the bat up in front of my face again, he let me know he wasn't leaving without what he wanted. Then he smiled and changed tactics. He turned to look at my friend. "String that one up.", he ordered. The other two cut his ropes and started dragging him over to another pipe.

That aide must have had some kind of revelation on the way to his beating cause he suddenly became a FIRST CLASS liar and probably saved BOTH our lives. That fellow broke down, blubbered, and just generally made up all KINDS of stuff.

He had a detailed, sensible answer for every question they asked! He even had ME so convinced, that I was mad as HELL at him for not saying anything SOONER! I was even mad at him for giving it all away! Seems like when you're hanging by your thumbs mad just comes easy.

Eventually I suppose they'd bought enough of what he said. Cutting me down, they drove us around for a while, then gave us both a first class rollout in another stinking alley in Da Nang. That was about the most memorable 24 hour pass I EVER got while I was in the Marines.

Some different fellows came a week or so later asking me about participating in an "action" that involved a lot of money on a military plane being intercepted by them.

I suppose it HAD to have been connected to that whole other mess somehow. Figuring they might be like those other boys, I gave them the politest "I'll have to think about that." I could "and got the hell out of there.

Figuring the whole thing had something to do with the CIA at the time, in retrospect I'm just not sure anymore.

———

Delivering papers wasn't all I did though. They'd have me go sort out shipping problems at the Bridge Ramp too for vehicles and parts for the transportation command.

One day they had me take a detail of men over there to hand load some items that needed special treatment. Special treatment was code for making sure one in three of whatever it was got set aside for "general use".

We got done in record time so the Captain told me to get these boys "taken care of." In my command that was code for a trip to what was affectionately referred to as "Dog Patch".

Dog Patch was an above averagely disreputable area that was plain old off limits to military personnel. Now don't get me wrong, there was a lot of restaurants, barbershops, stores, and other perfectly legitimate businesses there.

You HAD to say though, that it possessed MORE than it's fair share of what were rightly called the dregs of society. Prostitutes, gamblers, pimps, pushers, and worse all made their way through their own little pieces of hell there.

Some might say that one man's hell is another mans heaven. Marines being the sort to walk directly into hell with their safeties off and their bayonets fixed, a fair number of them just naturally couldn't resist a place like that. This in spite, and maybe BECAUSE, of the MP's sweeping through to pick up "government property" that managed to go astray there on a fairly regular basis.

Now you might not believe me when I say the whores didn't get me while I was in Vietnam, but it's true. You'll know better why a little later in my tale but Grandpa William had branded just enough preacher on my soul to avoid that particular vice just long enough. I'm sure he'd be proud to know it, and I was glad he did.

Begrudging the other fellows their "fun" when they insisted on having it wasn't a possibility though. You had to do things that rubbed you wrong all around just to get along there, and you GOT along because you never KNEW when your life was going to depend on one of these fellows being willing to come drag YOUR sorry busted up ass out of a serious fire.

So when the Captain said "fix them up" that's what I did. We put them in a truck and hauled them over to one of the more "reputable" Dog Patch joints. Reputable meant it was close to a military radar installation that was "home free" if you could get there before the MPs. That and nobody had been killed there recently.

Sitting in there with a glass of something with an umbrella in it, cooling my heels, I was brought around from my communion with the distiller's child by someone yelling "MPs!!" I heard those military dogs barking then. Orders or not, I knew the Captain couldn't cover me on this so I rolled those boys out WITH or WITHOUT pants 'cause we had to get GONE!

We all sprinted for the truck, and everybody piled in while I counted heads. Somebody was missing.

Now there was a black fellow we called Rudolph that was SUPPOSED to be helping me watch the BACKS of these other MARINES. Just then I spotted him shuffling out the door and it appeared he'd got caught up in the excitement. He'd managed to get his boots caught in his pants and was doing his absolute BEST to run with them all tangled around his ANKLES!

I'll never forget all of us cheering and yelling while he shuffled, hopped, and swore like a MANIAC trying to outrun a couple of military trained German Shepherds. At the last second one of the pants legs came free and he PUT on an extra burst of speed, just about getting to the tailgate as the truck started pulling away.

They were all trying to drag him into the truck when he let out a HOWL and leaped up in there, knocking everybody over. He'd got the help he needed and that DOG had got his pound of FLESH. We all made it to the Radar installation though.

As you can probably tell, it wasn't too uncommon for Marines stationed at Tien Shaw to get a little time in Da Nang. Another time I got done early at the deep water pier I decided to get me a cheeseburger at an enlisted club they had in Da Nang. I'd heard they did right by a half pound of ground beef about as good as anybody and son I was ANXIOUS to investigate that claim.

It took about two bites to get halfway through the first one and son, it was GOOD. Grinding on it some, I noticed an Army Sergeant watching me apparently amused. "Wa' hell son," he smiled, "are you hungry or whut?" "Yes sir I am." I puffed back at him around a mouthful of cheeseburger, "And I'm fixin ta need some ketchup!" He brought some over and just like that we got to talking.

Turned out he was from Vinegar Bend Alabama, which just about made us KIN over here. We talked about home and wishing for letters. I told him I'd only got one since I'd been here. "Wa' hell son!" he lamented, "Why don't you jus give 'em a caw?" I had to smile at that, and started explaining to him about phone lines until he interrupted, laughing. "Naw naw you idjit, a MARS call. You get over to the MARS station and you tell 'em Dibbs sentcha, they'll fix you right up!"

Wolfing down the rest of my food, I thanked him kindly, "owed him" one, and followed his directions to the MARS station. I didn't know exactly what part of Mars these boys were from, but if I got to talk to my family it was all the same to me!

I gotta say those MARS boys had a pretty nice hootch. It was all cinder blocks and concrete and cool as a cucumber inside. They even had a concrete patio with a BIG old barbecue welded up on the side. Dibbs' name was as good as gold with these fellows and they waved me in with a BIG smile when I mentioned it. I'm guessing he must have had something to do with that barbecue.

They had a couple of 65 foot radio towers that could get clear through to San Diego, and an operator there would dial through to whoever you wanted and hold the mike up to the phone as near as I could tell. It wasn't crystal clear, but any piece of home sounded about like heaven to me right now.

"Hello?", a faint high pitched voice came over the line. "Mama!", I cried, "It's me, your boy Bob!"

"Bob? Bobby boy! How are you doin' son, have you been shot? I read the news every day, but they don't say anything about you." I had to smile at that.

"Now I'm not sure I'm important enough for any headlines mama, but no I'm not shot. I'm just fine, just FINE!", I insisted, trying to maker her feel easy about me. A familiar noise sounded from off to the west and I cringed a little, waiting for the inevitable explosions to start.

"How are you mama?", I offered, not wanting the conversation to end just yet. "I'm just fine! The flowers are blooming and your fathers been spending some time around the house fixing things up." "Yes ma'am that sounds real good, how is Daddy anyway?"

She paused for a moment. "He's fine son.", she said in a slightly lower tone as the explosions at the perimeter of the camp started getting closer. Those MARS fellows took cover under their desks and such, but I wasn't going to let anything as common as a

MORTAR attack keep me from what I was sure was my one phone call home.

"What's that noise son?", she asked worriedly.

"Oh...nothing mama, they just practice with the guns a lot around here!", which was true. I didn't have to tell her it was the North Vietnamese practicing on us did I? An explosion shook the building.

About that time the operator in San Diego decided he'd better try to save my life. "Ummm...sir, those "practice" rounds sound like they're falling uhhh outside the range a little, maybe you'd better take cover anyway just in case." I sighed, "Yeah I reckon you're right."

"Well bobby, it's been just beautiful hearing your voice son!", she chirped. "Yes ma'am, I love you Mama! Say hi to Daddy and everybody for me!", I begged. "I will son," she promised, "Now you stay safe and don't you go marrying any of those black girls! I love you son!", she finished as the line clicked.

"Goodbye Mama...", I said to the already dead line, pausing to soak it in like the breath of fresh air it was. Another explosion brought me back to reality and I rolled under a desk, buried my face in the wall, and cried for the first time in years. 9000 miles away, my mama still had the power to make me happy and sad at the same time.

I thought I'd gotten out of reach of my mama but I guess I was glad to be wrong. Turns out that wasn't all she had the power to do either I found out later.

———

There was one thing I definitely didn't like about the war when I got there. Now there are of course, a LOT of bad things about war in general, but the thing that you never could really get away from was the NOISE! It seemed like it was ALWAYS noisy when you didn't want it to be. For a long time I couldn't sleep at Tien Shaw.

Those rockets came in about every night like they were on a schedule. I could just picture the VC up in the hills with a TV guide. One guy would say, "Oh look the 'Tonight Show' is over!" , and the other would say "Time for the rockets!"

Sometimes they'd switch up for variety and mortar us. We didn't take it without a fight either. The artillery and fifty caliber machine guns would run all night too. Sometimes they got the job done, sometimes they didn't. If those mortar batteries got TOO close some Marines got sent out to deal with it and usually got the job done. They'd bring back mortars and AK's from those trips since the owners didn't need them anymore.

Like I said, I reckon I acclimated to it after a while, actually getting to where I slept better when the 50 caliber machine guns were firing. If they stopped for longer than a few minute my eyes would pop open figuring that meant we were getting overrun, but then they'd start up again banging away at something on the perimeter, and I'd smile and go back to sleep.

You know I never did ask one of those heavy machine gunners, but I wouldn't be surprised if they popped off a belt or two every now and then just so people could sleep.

From my conversations with the Captain, I found out he lived in a little reinforced village called Song. It didn't take me long to figure out that he took a lot more transportation materials than any small Vietnamese village could possibly use. Like I said though, life was pretty cheap around this place so I decided to just keep my mouth shut, my ears open, and obey orders.

I guess he noticed my discretion and appreciated my cooperation 'cause after a few months he set me up with orders to change my base of operations. It looked like from now on I was going to be living in Song.

When I finally got posted to Song I thought I was going to enjoy the peace and quiet out there. Wouldn't you know it, I had a hard time getting used to how quiet it was in Song and couldn't sleep a wink for the first few days. It was almost like a vacation getting back to where the fifties were running all night when I did the maintenance runs.

SONG

I still had duties to perform and getting that old M-48 set up with maintenance was one of them. The M-48 was kind of a Korean war leftover but it was nice to have a real piece of artillery around anyhow. It wasn't very useful in the jungle because the treads just weren't wide enough for the weight. That thing would always get bogged down in the jungle dirt and would NOT turn on a dime in those trees. Captain Cong kept it in the middle of the village pointing out like an old cannon in a town square.

Even though we didn't use it much it needed work pretty frequently just 'cause that country wore down anything that would rust like you wouldn't believe. By now that old tank was just about held together with rust in parts so I got a crew together and dutifully loaded it up on the next LCU that came by.

Turns out THAT boat had an LST offshore waiting on it. Well that's the government for you I suppose. They drove out to that LST and loaded our boat in THAT boat for a six hour trip to Da Nang. We played cards with the LST crew on the way and I about lost my shorts so I was a little low on cash when we tied up to the deep water pier and got that tank off loaded.

A Captain met me there and assigned us to bunk with a couple of guys at the end of the ramp and that's where I met Paul. It seemed like just about everybody I knew in Vietnam was just trying to get through it, follow orders the best they could, and still have a life of some kind, so folks did all kinds of crazy things just to stay sane. Paul was no exception and we seemed to have a lot in common.

Well there wasn't much to do there after we got the tank off loaded so Paul and I just chewed the fat for a while, watching the Navy off load some supplies. A forklift came out of the hold of a cargo ship with pallet of beer, set it neatly down, and went back for another, and another, and ANOTHER! Before you knew it they had built the great wall of BEER, eighteen pallets long, three deep, and two high!,

Paul got to looking at this tremendous thirst quenching structure and figured out loud that the Navy owed us a six pack. Well I liked his thinking and told him I'd come back and get some later. He just nodded real slowly, which I took for as much permission as I needed.

Waiting for things on the pier to slow down a little, I went back and started walking around this huge mass of potential satisfaction. Lo and behold I found that some Navy boy had very kindly parked a forklift right behind my target! Well at this point it was just as easy to take a pallet as a six pack so I started it up and off I went with a little over four thousand cans of Budweiser!

Well it was ALL smiles when I rolled up to the tent, but there was no time for drinking 'cause we had to get this stuff out of sight. I ordered my crew to start digging so we could bury it and would you believe it, about four feet down they struck BALLANTINE. It seemed like somebody else had the same bright idea but no luck on the follow through so we were now in the middle of over EIGHT THOUSAND cans of beer!

We discussed putting together some kind of swimming pool to fill with it and buried the Budweiser the best we could, quickly breaking up the pallet and covering it with only less than a foot of sand.

That night was some serious rain, I mean it poured. I figured those cardboard cases would disintegrate and we'd have to pull out single cans but there wasn't anything to do about at this point except get some sleep.

The next morning I woke up to the sound of a horn outside the tent. Rolling out of the bunk, I took a look outside and it was some Captain in a Jeep hollering for me to come out. Throwing on a shirt and boots, I hustled out. About the second step down I got a can of beer under my boot and the next thing I knew my feet were flying and I landed in a foot of water.

Standing up the best I could, I put on a dripping salute and swiveled my eyes around to survey the scene. Turned out not only were we in a little bit of a low spot there around the hooch, but a few inches of sand will NOT hold down four thousand cans of Budweiser under water and I was literally
SWIMMING in BEER!

The cans rattled around my ankles as I walked slowly over to the Captains Jeep, trying my best to maintain a military demeanor. He ordered me to get the tank loaded on a trailer for transportation to a maintenance depot. It'd be about three days getting worked on.

"And Sergeant!" he frowned, "You better get your head out of your ass, and get rid of this beer by tonight!!" He slapped his driver on the shoulder and off they went. I rolled my boys out and we got those cans piled out of sight under a tarp.

Telling my crew that we were having us a BEER party as soon as we got the tank loaded up, there was no shortage of enthusiasm for the work. We got that metal beast trailered up in record time, and started pulling out cans, and rinsing them off for later. We'd got through about thirty, when somebody hollered the Harbor Master was coming!

We quickly camouflaged that beer can mountain the best we could and made a real show out of thoroughly cleaning the few cans we were working on. He walked by, took one look, and got about 4,000 cans worth of mad. Swearing more or less like...well...a sailor. He started yelling about court-martialing us if we didn't get those thirty cans to his office immediately! I guess they'd had more than just us pecking at their hops and he was on the war path about it.

Paul and I looked at each other. What could we say to that? Sounded like a pretty good deal to me, so I gave him my best "Aye Aye Sir!" and assigned one of my boys to haul those thirty cans to the harbor master while we continued getting the other 4,000 or so cans ready for what just about anybody would have to consider some pretty serious imbibing.

We put the word out and there was a fantastic beer bash that night featuring about every kind of Private, Corporal, Sergeant, and Vietnamese civilian you can imagine with a few more ale guzzling oddities beside. I think that included a couple of dogs and a goat even.

It got crazy enough that there were probably some VC drinking with us but nobody cared that night.

That Captain found a generous share in a convenient spot as well. I figured in this case it was a matter of leading from the front since he'd wanted us to get rid of the beer.

It took us about the whole three days to recover from that operation, but we were ready to roll by the time the tank got back. There were still thousands of cans of Ballantine so I consulted with Paul then took the tank for a little "test drive" down next to the hootch. I figured nobody would notice an extra quarter ton or so in a forty five ton tank so we loaded a small share in it.

I made a point of providing a generous Ballantine basket to the Navy for their transportation services when they dropped us off at song. You can imagine we were sorely missed by the Navy and pretty well welcomed back to by the majority of the village.

Other than the maintenance trips to Bridge ramp and the odd assignments for the transportation command at the deep water pier, Life at Song was pretty quiet.

It was a small, I would even say picturesque, farm village on the coast South of Hue, with around a hundred souls. I inspected and bolstered their defenses, ordered received and inventoried U.S. property, and trained their soldiers.

Song, as I said, was a reinforced village that Captain
Cong happened to live in. His family, and the wives
and children of his soldiers, all lived there pretty much
in peace.

Unfortunately, Song was on the main road in that area
that wove in and out of the jungle along the shoreline.
The Captain and I both knew their peace wouldn't last.
Villages like this were snuffed out regularly to deny
bases of operation to the Americans, and to punish
collaborators.

The punishment was often inhumanly monstrous.
Being skinned and burned alive happened regularly. I
heard one time a Montagnard village, mostly women
and children, even infants, were all burned to death
with flame throwers because they wouldn't help carry
ammunition for the VC.

Maybe worse was being sent to the NVA "reeducation"
camps where a bunch died of disease, malnutrition,
plain old lead poisoning, and whatever else the NVA
imagined up.

 The worst excesses you may have heard about
American forces, bad as they were, were like a church
picnic compared to the scale, regularity, and sheer
viciousness the Godless VC were capable of. Don't let
anybody tell you different. Anyone that spent some
real time there knows. Pieces of their "patriot forces"
could be found chained to their weapons or shackled in
the burnt out hulls of tanks when battles were over.

I honestly felt like I was doing the world a favor every

time I dropped one of those bastards. It felt good. I've been unable to feel ANYTHING but right about what I did to the North Vietnamese Soldiers for the South Vietnamese Separatists during the war and I don't understand men who don't.

The villagers in Song were mostly Catholic. There was a tiny church with it's own Priest, and an orphanage. The South Vietnamese who most strongly wanted to separate from the North were largely Catholic. This made them a bit more humane than the North Vietnamese, but not a lot.

I didn't start on patrols for a while after arriving since I was the only American there and valuable, because with me came American supplies, guns, and ammunition. I'd studied the maps of the surrounding terrain though, and was doing everything I could in training and defense. Best of all though, and I don't how Captain Cong swung it, we got ourselves an Ontos tank!

The Ontos was, and STILL holds the record in my book as, the world's NASTIEST shotgun! Six 106mm recoilless cannons mounted on a light armored tank chassis with nice wide tracks for soft dirt.

You could fire any 106mm shell but the favorite was a flechette round called "beehive". When you let loose all six guns at once, the earth shook, the jungle in front of that beast was cleared of every living creature in a cone about 1500 feet long, and anything behind it for about 30 feet got incinerated. It was one of the few weapons we had the VC were REALLY scared of.

Seeing as how I'd never driven a tank, naturally it was my job to go pick it up at the Deep Water Pier. The Captain called me in one day and told me I was his new tank driver! He explained the situation and as usual I said "Yes Sir" and got on with it.

Me and Lieutenant Loo both went on that expedition since he had some business in Da Nang, so we got a jeep and spun off to highway one.

Pulling out the papers the Captain had given me; I sorted out where it was and found my way over. When I told the man in charge what I was after, he took me to the beast, opened the drivers hatch on it and said "Good luck!" Just like that I was a tank driver.

I'd driven a tractor a time or two so I didn't figure this'd be much worse. Managing to get it started I played with the steering levers a little, and then made a few tentative little starts.

Figuring I'd better just get it done, I grabbed those sticks and shoved 'em forward and just like THAT I was a tank driver. Brakes weren't a problem cause eight tons on tracks doesn't coast too well. Kind of wobbling my way down the peer I managed to bump into stuff a little and scatter some people but I got it over to the bridge ramp anyway.

I never did figure out why in the world they had it on the Deep Water Pier in the first place. Getting on an LST at Bridge Ramp, we floated her on up to Song.

138

The Captain liked to mainly have it sit in plain sight pointed at the jungle to give 'em something to think about.

As the American attaché one of my jobs was to deliver it for maintenance up the coast whenever needed so I got pretty familiar with it. It wasn't hard to drive and the guns could fire singly or all at once using buttons under the commander's hatch, but you could reach them from the driver's seat if you stretched.

There was a pedal that operated a fifty caliber gun with tracer rounds for targeting. I hear some of them had thirty caliber machine guns but I never saw one. We had the Ontos and the older m48 tank that was in fair shape and well supplied.

The area around the village was pretty much cleared except for rice paddies with paths winding between them. Any attacks would have to cross between one and two thousand feet of pretty much open space.

It was as secure a location as you could get. We had the water at our backs, plenty of room to spot an attack, some serious artillery, and the Air Cav had promised us choppers on call. I'm guessing Captain Cong began to wish he'd he'd spent his clout on an LCU before the end. I'm not sure it would've mattered though.

The first week I was there he invited me to dinner with his family. He had a lovely, petite wife, and two young children. I recall her being an excellent cook and, as it turns out, a pretty fair matchmaker. She had all the officers to those dinners and made sure there was an eligible bachelorette sitting next to every bachelor whenever she could.

They even had a little sort of swearing in ceremony for me. Captain Cong pinned some Lieutenant bars on me right there for all his other officers to see! He even made a little speech about their American allies!

More importantly, that's where I was introduced to Kim.

Kim was the most beautiful, and delicate thing I'd ever seen. She ran the orphanage there, and was considered a Saint by the villagers. I have to say I was in that number. She was as good a person as that country ever produced.

I'm not saying she didn't have any fire in her. Once I got to know her better, in some ways she reminded me of my Mama. When she or my Mama got their back up about something you'd better stand down until it blew over or you were liable to suffer as I recall. At first I thought it was the war that had made her a strong woman.

She'd even been educated in the US, with a Nursing degree from Boston College, and was impressed that I spoke Vietnamese so well. That was fortunate, since I don't recall there being a lot else about me to impress as fine a woman as she seemed to me.

It wasn't a particularly big orphanage with little over a dozen children, but I made sure to reinforce it with barrels of dirt along the walls and more than one way to escape. Those children might or might not die in an attack, but there was no way on Gods green Earth it was going to be my fault, and I especially wanted to please Kim.

That orphanage would be the last place to fall as far as I was concerned and I set up defenses around it based on that. There were enough claymores and crossfire to choke a herd of elephants around that building, but I made sure it was obvious it was an orphanage in hopes that any VC attack might show a little mercy. They did like to carry off children and make soldiers out of them sometimes, and I hoped they'd want them alive rather than dead like the rest of us.

I'll confess to arranging to spend as much time as possible strengthening the orphanage, teaching classes, and just plain playing with those children, all just so I could have a chance to show off for Kim.

I taught them basketball using some old kickball's and even got a little bit of a league going. It wasn't much to watch, but it was fun! There was one little boy named Phien that really took to it, and loved to show off, when he did something new. He'd yell, "Look Lieutenant Bob look! You look now!".

I learned to love those children, and sometimes I'd catch Kim looking at me in a way I'd secretly crave. When she was happy, I was happy. When she was sad, I was sad.

The dinners together at Captain Cong's home became a treat I looked forward to, and sometimes we would take walks down to the beach. That's where she told me about her parents in Saigon, her life before Song, and her time in the U.S. . That's where she listened to my stories.

It was where we first kissed.

The war had a way of getting between a man and his social life though. While I was chasing her or being chased (I was never sure which) there was plenty to do. Some of it was more exciting than the other, but it ALL had to get done.

We were sitting on that same beach one evening, holding hands and looking at the sun set when she started describing her dream home to me. "Shutters," she insisted, "green shutters, and the trim should be green too. I love those green metal roofs."

She paused for a moment, glancing at me, then continued, "The kitchen doesn't have to be very big, but I'd like a separate dining area that connects to the living room. A hallway to two bedrooms would be nice. We'd need an extra bedroom for children."

When I heard that "We" I about rolled off my chair! Looking over at her, all I could stutter (it still happened sometimes) was "W-w-w-we?"

"Well sure, why not?", she smiled at me. "It's a dream right?"

———

I thought about that for a moment, calculating and putting a few things together in my head. "I could build that for you." I insisted quietly.

MARK 12-7

She looked at me, surprised, and then I saw something in her eye's I hadn't seen before. The were glistening and soft as she reached out and squeezed my hand gently. "Really?" she asked quietly.

Well boy I tell you what, I knew it was now or never and I got down on one knee and begged her to marry me the best way I knew how. I can't remember my speech since I hadn't exactly prepared one, but I definitely remember saying "please" about half a dozen times. I must have been a pitiful sight.

She put a hand over her mouth and laughed. For a second I thought she was laughing at me, but then she took my other hand and drew me closer. "Of course I will!", she insisted brightly, giggling a little as she kissed me.

It was my turn to laugh out loud now. We laughed and she cried, and I'll admit I teared up a little myself, happier than I'd ever been my whole life.

"Oh Robert!," she sobbed, "I can hardly wait to introduce you to my parents!" Well my happy meter dropped a notch at that, and I gulped a little. Feeling the way I did though, I could face a lion with a pocket knife if it meant I could get started on that house.

Knowing I had to be completely honest with her from day one, I discussed my parents with her immediately. It was a tremendous relief that she actually thought it was funny that my mama thought the Vietnamese were African.

I did my best to give her, the reality, telling her, my dad was a pretty even minded man, and would love whoever I loved; my mama might need some convincing though. She brushed it aside, convinced that her personal charm and native intelligence would be enough to win her over. "You'd better brush up on those before you meet my mother." , I laughed, happy she was taking as much of my parents as I could introduce so well.

We agreed that after we got married we'd take a trip to the U.S. as soon as we could to introduce her.

The day after I popped the question and got my yes, we started discussing details. Well when I say "discussed" what I mean is like any good fiancée, she told me the details, and I said "Yes ma'am." After all this really was her big day and I was at least smart enough to know that and let her have it all. I was a pretty fair hand with an ambush or fire formations, but she was definitely closer to being a marriage planner than I'd ever be for sure.

We talked about going to see HER parents in Saigon. Naturally I was a little nervous about meeting them so

I tried to find out more about the opposition there. "What exactly do they do again?" I asked, feeling like I'd missed something.

"They own a few restaurants." she reminded me quietly. Well of course that didn't sound too bad. I supposed we'd get some good meals there anyway.

You know, most fellows would be worried about meeting the dad, but Kim talked so much about her mom. Her mom got them into the restaurant business. Her mom talked her dad out of his farm and into the restaurant business. Her mom did this. Her mom did that. I started getting a little worried about what her mom might do when we showed up!

We announced our engagement to Captain Cong who smiled the broadest I'd ever seen and shook my hand heartily. His wife was very happy for us too. They threw us a real feast that weekend and I had no trouble getting the weeks leave to go with Kim to Saigon, and a Jeep to boot!

When we pulled up to that vast, white columned, French colonial mansion her parents lived in, I knew Kim had been buttering my bread on both sides. Owned a few restaurants...right. I found out later that they owned ALL the concession franchises for every American military base in Vietnam. Nobody sold so much as a potato chip to an American serviceman unless they got their cut, and I tell you what, it amounted to some.

She smiled at me when she saw my reaction, and I

knew she'd been holding back to make sure of me. "Don't worry, they're very nice!" she smiled, reaching out a hand, "They're going to love you."

"Exactly how do you know that?" I remember asking nervously as I eyed the imposing structure she was proposing to invade.

"Because," she smiled again, snuggling under my arm, "I do."

So I walked into the jaws of the white lion. Fortunately, her parents were real nice just like she'd said. They were surprised at how good my Vietnamese was too.

Honestly, that was something that still surprised me sometimes. The more I felt that, the more it became obvious that was something I was meant to do. It was a big part of the reason I'd survived here, the reason I'd met Kim, and now the reason I was meeting her parents.

Well that was how "hello" went anyway; it was a real wrestling match after that.

The first sticking point was religion. My Baptist faith went over like a mugging with their Catholic sensibilities. Her mother didn't miss a lick though,"Well," she smoothed over all Protestantism with a single stroke,"…you can convert." That was the end of my faith as far as she was concerned.

Her father was not just a little reticent about me in

general I could tell, but I couldn't blame him for that. Having a lot of sisters, I'd seen that before and even felt for him some. Telling him so broke the ice nicely there. Still, it was her mother that took the lions share of the inquisition.

As restaurateurs they dealt with a lot of farmers, and he hadn't just had a farm, he'd had his own rubber plantation. My family having so many hundreds of acres and my Grandpa, having been a farmer, made the right impression on them. They were pleased to find he'd been a preaching man too in spite of his apparently misguided spirituality. I think they pictured him in a white suit with a string bow tie on the veranda sipping a mint julep then changing into white collared vestry for Sundays.

My father's secret work with the Air Force involving cameras made a real dent on them too. I always loved telling people that and watching their minds work on a fiction that was probably better than the facts. The truth was, of course, that I really didn't know any more about it than they did.

Then they asked me what I wanted to do.

Staying alive had occupied my time so well I hadn't thought ahead a whole lot and I'm sure I got a deer in the headlights look for a second there. Survival sounded pretty good to me, but I figured that's not what they wanted to hear. "I was considering staying in the Corp." I ventured, seeing their faces freeze for a second I added quickly, "…but I don't have any definite plans yet."

Her mother appeared to like that and she forged ahead with a whole set of plans for me that I was bright enough to nod my head to whether I liked them or not. Apparently we were going to kick the VC back into North Vietnam permanently, Kim and I were going to move to Saigon, and I was going to help them squeeze money out of the franchises. Not being strictly against money, it sounded ok to me so far on theory.

"Well…", Kim interrupted just after we'd had their third theoretical grandchild, "I'm going to stay at the orphanage for a while.", then dug back into her plate like nothing had happened.

Her mother stopped with her mouth open for a moment. "Well we'll see about that.", she dismissed her daughter as easily as she had every Baptist in the world, then changed the subject back to our well documented future.

Glancing at her father, I noticed him watching me with an almost amused look as he took another purposeful bite, chewing very thoughtfully. I was right about her mother. I'd have liked to see her and my mama go a few rounds just out of morbid curiosity. My mother was a real force of nature but this lady might have matched her.

The other thing I was right on about was the FOOD. That was for sure the best I'd ever eaten in my life both Vietnamese, American, and I'll add French cuisine. They brought out the works and the kitchen sink to put it in. I almost started getting concerned whether or not

---

148

there'd be any left for the wedding, but every time it occurred to me they brought out another course to ease my mind.

Kim was right as it turned out. I was Christian enough to make them comfortable, and man enough to get their approval. Shaking hands with her father as we left and seeing the look in his eyes, I knew I'd made my mark on a man of quality.

On the drive back home I realized I had the men of quality in my family to thank for it. That was a good day for me.

With what I THOUGHT was the biggest hurdle out of the way, the drive back to Song was just about a dream. Kim and I held hands all the way there and words weren't even necessary. The beauty of Vietnam stood out to me and I hardly noticed any burned out buildings or shell craters, and it only occurred to me once that we might be less likely to be attacked because I had a Vietnamese woman in the jeep with me.

It was only bettered by the day we married. One of my biggest regrets in life is that it didn't come sooner.

Having collected a lot of personal items by then, I decided to pack some of them in a trunk and ship it home, making sure to put a picture of Kim and some of our letters in there. That way even if I didn't make it they'd know.

There was no way to tell when I'd see them, but I knew

I had to tell them in person. They'd only written me two letters while I was in Vietnam so it wasn't like they were expecting me to write anyway. Maybe that was just another excuse to put it off though.

I would just as soon have gotten married right away but her parents insisted on us waiting a few months. Throwing myself into my duties and getting a home built for us in song, I managed to keep busy.

Captain Cong sent for me to report to him in his office. When I got there Captain Cong handed me a letter from home, I set there and read the letter, and mom described how sick dad was, and wanted me to come home as quickly as possible.

Taking the letter back to the orphanage, I sat there with my head in my hands as Kim read and considered it. We discussed her going with me, but of course that was out of the question since it might cause more stress for my dad (by way of my mother) and she had the orphanage to run.

"Kim…", I started hesitantly, "I'm not sure it's a good idea for me to…to tell them." I hung my head, ashamed of myself, and embarrassed to say anything like that to my own future wife.

Well, I explained to her about daddy's condition and went back over my Mama's probable reaction to our impending marriage, and one thing the Vietnamese understand is family. Relenting on that was easy for her.

We hadn't exactly set a date yet but I didn't mind too much. I was riding pretty high from what I'd taken for acceptance from her family and was just pleased to be happy for the short time I had between then and when I heard about Daddy.

Well when it rains it pours and though she was pretty even minded about the trip I had to take, she didn't take AT ALL to the next idea I proposed. It made all the sense in the world to me, but she wasn't having any. I should have known better from how she stood her mother up on the subject of moving to Saigon.

Diving right in on the subject of her coming to live in Utah or California, I kind of figured out loud that I might get a stateside posting and we could get away from there.

I guess she'd gotten used to pushing people around to get what she could for those orphans. I'd heard her call folks "MISTER whoever" whenever she needed a box of something or special favor. Well she gave me the "MISTER Mizell" then. There were times after that I gave in and times I didn't, but I was for danged sure I didn't want to get called out like that very often after the first time.

She didn't yell, but she laid it out for me then. You can imagine we got to talking about where we wanted to live. In my ignorance and I've got to say naïveté I just assumed she wanted to go to the U.S. with me.

She'd lived over there after all and had to know how much better it was in the states. She was an only child anyway and her parents were just plain RICH and could come see us whenever they wanted! How could you want to stay somewhere you could wake up dead just about any day of the week!?

Listen to me go on. I guess I'm still trying to change things. You just never stop having some arguments with yourself I suppose, and son we had one then.

Like I said, yelling wasn't her way, but she stood her ground. Thinking back, if she could stand up to that mother of hers I should've known there wasn't half a chance for a small town victim of the suburbs like me. She cared about that orphanage and those kids about even with me and she let me know it, letting on she didn't really know what she'd decide if I forced that on her.

It didn't seem like much of an argument to me, but I'd never seen her that angry before so I took it to heart. The next thing she said left me a little cold inside, "Mister Mizell, you need to go home and decide where you want to live."

My heart sank when it finally and fully impacted on me. I knew I wasn't leaving Kim there by herself.

"Vietnam..."

It was about all I could do to blink that night. When the sun finally came up it was about the same, and there it was again.

"Vietnam!?"

Thinking about daddy, mama, all my brothers and sisters, Grandma, and everything I'd ever liked about life before the Marines, son I can tell you it tore me up. Figuring I needed some time away from her to think, I begged the Captain for some kind of work at Hue and he gave it to me. We more or less made up some little thing that needed doing and called a boat in.

Not wanting Kim to take my leaving too hard, I made sure to give her the best goodbye I knew how before I drove that jeep up into the LCU for the trip to Hue, telling her I'd be back soon.

There were a lot of Americans that plain old shacked up with women in Vietnam and had a regular day job with the military. You weren't supposed too but they did it anyway and people just looked the other way.

That wasn't for me though. Kim, and me, wanted the same thing there, a home, family, a real life. Apparently we just wanted the same thing on about opposite sides of the planet.

Dropping off the jeep, I took a bunk at Tien Shaw and set about thinking. Well that didn't work any better here than there and some walking around was in order.

Drifting over to the mess hall I saw what you'd have to say was an unusually large crowd gathered at the Recreational hall. I was ready for anything to take my mind of Kim for a minute, so I poked my head in.

I had to jostle a little to get a decent look and I wasn't

153

sure what I was looking at even when I DID. It looked like a fellow in a diving suit only there wasn't any water.

"What's the big deal?", I asked somebody there and that fellow looked at me like I was from Mars. "You been living under a rock or something? That's Neil Armstrong, he's about to step onto the f****** MOON!"

Son, you could have knocked me over, with a twig! That was the first time I'd heard anything about a trip to the moon. I don't know how I'd missed that news but I guess I had.

He took that little jump off the ladder and said it, "One small step for a man, and one giant leap for mankind." I don't remember if it was live or not, but I tell you what, we made some NOISE then.

An American on the moon!

The coverage continued as they shuffled and hopped around on the moon. I couldn't stop watching! I guess most of these other fellows had been following this stuff already cause they all went to eat after a while.

Sitting there, watching one of our boys prancing around in a crater on the moon, I didn't feel so far from home anymore. America was just right around the corner.

That night I looked up at the moon and thought about Kim. For the first time I thought to myself,

"Well...why not?"

Requesting permission to return home on leave, wasn't a problem, I was nearing the end of my first tour, which I extended , and Permission was granted, the request went up the chain, and I got my orders to report to Da Nang for a flight connecting through Okinawa within a few days.

The flight was a little rough, but those Air Force boys always acted like they'd let somebody down if they hadn't made somebody puke while they were flying non-coms and regular GI's around. I did my best not to give them the satisfaction, but nature just hadn't intended for my stomach to be jerked around that far in the air. I'm ashamed to say they got another notch on their wall before I got off.

Getting on another flight as quick as I could, I was in Salt Lake before Noon on a Tuesday as I recall. I hopped a cab at the airport, so mom and dad would not have to drive all the way to Salt Lake, I told the cab to stop just before he got to the house, so I could surprise, mom, and dad. When I opened the door there was dad setting in his chair at home, with mom watching T.V. in their Sunday best waiting for me to call them to pick me up, Dad told me to come outside for a minute, We went outside , dad told me he had to stop smoking, and he would have to have a heart operation, as soon as his health improved. Well, I knew my dad had been raised by a tough old man, so I was certain he would make it through this.

I remembered him at the airport saying goodbye, now it was my turn to cry a little. Dad asked if I was ok, I smiled back, putting my hand on his shoulder, saying never felt better.

"Mom told dad, you better get well quick John," she said, "I'm not gonna stay in this house without you." I'd never really seen how much she loved my father before. At that moment I had an overwhelming urge to just blurt out my secret, my marriage. Knowing I felt the same way about Kim. I bit my tongue though.

My mama was after me with all kinds of excuses and reasons to try and get stateside duty or some such. I practically had to tie her up to get out of the house and make the flight back to San Diego. Before you knew it though, my dad was doing better at home and I was on a flight to Vietnam.

OKINANAWA

Gratefully the flight back wasn't as exciting as the one out and we wound up in Okinawa at one point. I was called into a Captains office and was told my orders had changed. "They what?!" I managed. He informed me that he was holding a piece of paper saying that I was staying in Okinawa!

I suppose that Captain might have been confused by what must have seemed like my unreasonable desire to get back to Vietnam. From his point of view I'd been given a ticket a lot of Marines wished for. I had about nine months left in my enlistment and I was getting a chance to sit it out without having to worry about a rocket landing on my head while I was sleeping or a sniper putting a round between my shoulder blades while I was going about my business.

Spinning up every reason I could think of for getting back on that plane didn't make a dent in that man. "I didn't make these orders Sergeant, but I'm passing them on now and that's it. Go to the Gunny for a bunk and come back in tomorrow for your assignment. "

The real reasons I wanted to get back were exactly what I couldn't tell anybody of course. Kim was waiting for me back in Vietnam and in danger of rockets and mortars herself. I'd already about gone crazy wanting to get back to her once I knew dad was all right, and now this.

Leaving the Captain I immediately found a telegraph office and shot off a message to Captain Cong at ARVN transportation command that I knew he'd pass on to Kim. I tried to be comforting, but there's not much love letter you can put in something going through your commanding officer with about every other word being STOP.   Managing to let her know this was going to be as temporary as I could make it was about the best I could do.

———

Once I got that out of the way I wandered over to what passed for a watering hole there and discovered the little piece of magic that was going to get me through it. I begged the bartender to put me under and he smiled, did a little mixing and handed me my miracle.

The Singapore Sling.

Now I don't drink any more, and there's not much drinking I'm proud of, but I tell you what, they mixed slings like nobody else on Okinawa. A couple of those would make you hit the floor so fast you wouldn't even know your head was spinning before your skull hit the wood.

Being my first experience with this particular exotic treat, the next thing I knew was waking up with a fairly serious hangover in a bunk I didn't remember getting into. I rolled out as quickly as I could and got back over to the company office for my orders. Turns out I was now an MP.

Now I've heard since that the base in Okinawa got pretty wild about five or so years later with race riots, a SERIOUS drug problem, and all kinds of other craziness, but it wasn't like that when I was there.

Not that there weren't any problems. The REASON I was an MP was they needed some cause three Mp's had been dumped DEAD at the base gates by the locals just a few days before I got there. That was another piece of news I could've done without, but it definitely kept me on my toes.

Turned out even then the Okinawans had a serious problem with the Marine base there and at least some of them were willing to kill Marines over it. Those dead MPs were the end of a storm though and my time there passed pretty uneventfully.

About a month into it I was riding the base perimeter with a private when we noticed what looked for the entire world like somebody beating up a hooker. He had his hands on her throat and was shaking her like a dog when we showed up and she was gagging and wailing like the world was coming to an end.

Turns out he was trying to get his money back and she would be damned if he was getting back a penny. Now being who I was it was pretty natural for me to lack any sympathy for that fellow and I started off pushing on him pretty good. He wanted me to get his money back and I wasn't going to do it and was about certain he could count on me to kick his ass clean out the front gate if he so much as looked at me wrong at this point.

Then he dropped his little bomb shell, "Sir," he said, drawing himself up as best he could drunk, "I am the Japanese ambassador!"

Oh good lord.

At this point I'd had enough of both of them and told him he better get his ass off my base before I took a stick to him. True to my form though, I gave the lady a head start and let her keep the mans money anyway,

---

which made "The Ambassador" none to happy. I didn't speak Japanese, but I could guess what he was spewing at me as we watched that whore scramble out of sight, laughing and waving his money as she ran.

Well, it turned out he WAS the Japanese Ambassador. I suppose he didn't want this all getting out so nothing came of it, though I was a little tense for a couple of days waiting for the other shoe to drop.

Other than that I soldiered on the best I could. I wrote letters, sent telegrams, and did whatever I could to stay in touch with Kim, got through my watches as an MP, and drank myself stiff with Singapore slings.

It was so depressing that after a month or so I got on the phone to mama, hoping like any good son that she could make it better somehow. Turns out that couldn't have been further from the truth.

I put on how pitiful I was not being back with my command in Vietnam and generally danced all around the real reason. Mama hesitated, then told me something that hit me like a slap in the face, "Son", she said, "I just thought you'd be safer there."

"What?", was all the brilliant comment I could get out at that. What had my mother done now? Well she spilled the beans then and it turned out my dad wasn't the only one getting on base.

My mother had been attending a LOT of official functions and made a LOT of friends in high places. I guess her smooth Southern charm had won them over in Utah. Little did they know.

She had used every connection she had and somehow managed to get me held up in Okinawa. I never got exactly who she'd signed on to her pity party, but it got the job done. There I was 2,000 miles away from my pretty young wife.

I can't blame her much since dads health was precarious enough that any bad news about me might just push him over the edge. I didn't want that any more than she did but I HAD to get back to Vietnam.

Rolling my eyes, I thanked her best I could, said good bye, and started wracking my brains on how to get back. Now that I knew what was going on maybe I could work some angle at the company office.

I got over there and worked that Captain every way I could think of. Telling him what my mother had done, I begged myself blind for any kind of loophole there was light on the other side of. I went there every week and sometimes daily until he finally threw me a line.

"Well," he said, with about half a grin on his face, "actually there is one option." He wrote me a note and told me to take it to the recruiter.

I wasn't sure what he had in mind, but I got over there and handed it off to the officer in charge. He took a look and then sort of squinted at me. "So you want to re-enlist?" he asked.

If he'd slapped me I'd have sounded less surprised, "I

what?!"

"Re-enlist." he insisted, "that's what it says here."

Well I was so desperate by now that I was willing to listen to anything so I begged for details. Turned out if I signed up for another two years, they'd give me a pass on my remaining six months in my current enlistment (I'd been in Okinawa three months by then) and I'd be out in two years from that date.

I had to think about it for the rest of the week, and even wrote Kim a letter explaining the situation. She wrote back saying that was fine with her if it seemed wise to me. Marching back into the company office, I signed another two year enlistment and waited to be ordered back to Vietnam.

It didn't take long. Within a week I was flying back to the fiancée I'd won, the house I'd build with my own hands, and the people I'd cast my lot in with. I was going back to Song.

Of course my mama thought I'd lost my mind, but I suppose there's a time to cut the apron strings, and this was it for me. Of course I was going from one set to the other, but it was the right thing to do, and I knew it.

I was back at Song inside of a week. I'd like to say we got married right away but her parents made her put it off again for some reason or another. Maybe Kim wanted to make sure I was staying. Figuring the best way to solve that problem was to get that HOUSE built, I got on it son! It was starting to get cold anyway, and the thought of being in a nice cozy house with Kim that winter got me downright MOTIVATED!

Figuring I needed to do some old fashioned scrounging, I made sure to get every duty posting I could in Da Nang and Hue so I could be where that kind of action is.

Like I said before, my mama had no idea what kind of trouble she was getting me into when she got me stuck on Okinawa. That little MP tick on my paperwork got me volunteered for MP duty about half the time I went on any kind of duty in Hue or Da Nang. Half THOSE times they'd hold me over a few days so I was delayed getting back.

What could I do though, I WAS on loan to the Vietnamese, but I was the PROPERTY of the United States Marines. I made sure to let Captain Cong know and he always understood.

After one of those many night watches I was laid out on my rack at the air base, sawing away, when the ammo dump went up! To tell you how used I'd gotten to the noise, I didn't even wake up when the first explosions went off. What woke me was coughing from the thick dust flying around. I tell you what, I mean THICK. I tell you what; it's what I always thought an Oklahoma dust storm was like. You couldn't see your hand in front of your face sometimes.

I rolled out and could make out people running all over

the place. Stepping out of the tent, there was immediately another GIGANTIC explosion! I mean I THOUGHT I'd heard some noise and seen some stuff blow up, but never like THIS!

There'd be a HUGE flash, the ground would shake like an EARTHQUAKE and EVERYBODY would get KNOCKED on their ass! Then if you were lucky you might see the mushroom cloud and the shockwave would blow things over or knock you down AGAIN if you hadn't hit the dirt!

I tell you what; it was like boxing Joe Frazier, if you went down hard, you better stay down 'til the action was over. You could even see buildings popping like balloons sometimes, while the mushroom clouds shot up what HAD to have been HUNDREDS of feet.

 About every minute or so you'd see another one coming at you, then the mushroom cloud. Then you got knocked over again. Everybody would get up and run as far as they could between shockwaves. It didn't take long for me to feel sorry for anybody that was closer than I was.

I ran back into the hootch and started grabbing a few things. About the NEXT explosion the roof started comin' off that so I just LEFT the rest and got myself gone the best way I could find.

Well that didn't last long. As soon as the Gunny found me I was volunteered to stay for the whole show to keep the premises secure while everybody else up and left.

That was a real show I've got to say. When those big bombs on the Air Force side started going off, blowing I guess at least 50 foot holes in the ground, and shells were going off on the Marine side it got REALLY intense. Sheets of fire, mushroom clouds, and red hot metal rained everywhere.

We backed off about a number of miles and stood watch while the dump blew itself out. I guess it was a little later in the day, we'd gotten used to bouncing around and I even slept some.

I tell you what though, sometime during the day there was a BIG explosion. I mean it shot us up off the ground and bounced us around the inside of that bunker like we were ping pong balls! The timbers in that bunker cracked, dust and dirt was flying and we were just plain scared for a our lives!

Then this just VICIOUS shockwave rolled by knocking over towers and blowing the roof off some nearby buildings and even knocking one over. Now remember we had to have been at LEAST a MILE or two away from this stuff.

We ran out to look after stuff stopped falling on our location and there was world war three son. I guess that's about the closest you can get to an atom bomb without your skin melting off. There was this mushroom cloud maybe a thousand feet up in the sky, and it boiled and burned from top to bottom like every piece of hell I'd ever heard my Grandpa go on about!

I heard later something like a couple hundred
THOUSAND STICKS of DYNAMITE had went off
all at once. Well I'd thought those Air Force thousand
pound bombs going and 155 artillery shells shooting
off in random directions was entertaining, but after that
I was plain old ready to get off the ride and LEAVE
the PARK!

Sometime the next morning the detonations weren't as
bad or frequent so folks started coming back to clean
up. They let me back off the hook a few days later
then, so I GLADLY picked up the stuff I'd been
waiting on at the deep water pier, got it where it
needed going, and caught an ride back to Song.

For that and a lot of other reasons you can easily
imagine, I don't care for fireworks so much anymore.

Cory

When it started in toward winter we about always had
some kind of fire going during the nights in Song. If
there's anything close to something every human being
likes doing at any particular time it's definitely sitting
by a fire. A close second would be poking at it with a
stick.

During one night watch there in the village I'd got over
to the fire. Naturally I'd picked up a stick and started
poking at it.

About then an American just walked up and sat down next to me, just like that! He didn't even look at me, just stared at the fire. Song was NOT a big village and I knew everybody's face and just about everybody's name. This fellow was NOT on the list.

I immediately knew he hadn't come through the sentry points 'cause they'd have stopped him and informed me. That hadn't happened so I knew he'd come in through the perimeter which was plenty dangerous. I'd placed a lot of those claymores myself.

We'd even shot a half dozen or so fellows trying to get at us through the wire or trying to fool with the claymores in the last few months, but THERE HE WAS!

He had on ARVN jungle fatigues without a unit mark of any kind on them and wasn't a very big fellow. Well, he was bigger than me, but then about everybody was then and still are now.

Well now, I SAY he was an American. He could have been Russian or French or some such. There just weren't to many white guys wearing jungle fatigues in Vietnam that weren't American is all.

One thing was for sure though, having seen a LOT of killers there, I'd gotten to where I could tell the real deal, the real man hunters, and he was it. I can't explain it. You can just tell about some people, kind of see it in their eyes and in the way they move.

———

Figuring he must be some kind of Special Forces trying to make a statement about my defenses, I decided not to say a damned thing. We just sat and looked at the fire. He grabbed a stick and poked at it some.

A half hour later he got up and left without saying a word. I wasn't going to give him the satisfaction of acting like I cared so I just sat there and let him go.

Asking the sentries about it later, just like I expected they hadn't seen or heard a thing the whole night. Like I said, the real deal.

I told Kim about it but she just sort of waved it off and asked about the house. We couldn't really build what she wanted here since there wasn't much space, and she did really want to wind up in Saigon near her parents eventually.

Well if there's anything an in country Marine knows how to do it's SCROUNGE. I pulled in every favor, out and out absconded with some stuff, and even threatened a few people. By the time I'd gotten all that out of my system I'd scrounged up every piece of plywood and framing material I could find and had a very respectable stack of lumber.

One thing I remembered was she wanted a green tin roof, and I put out every feeler I had for some green tin. I finally got the word on some, got Captain Cong to work out a truck with the transportation command and drove all the way to Saigon to get it!

That's where I met Warrant Officer Ron Dowell. U.S. ARMY

Ron was the fellow one of those boys at the transportation command had told me about. He had every kind of construction material you could think of according to them. It took me about two seconds to decide the trip was worth it.

Making my way to his house, it was easy to see why everybody thought Ron was the MAN. He was set up like nobodies business. He'd got his self one of those French mansions close to the beach and customized it. He'd even built a concrete waterway all the way to the ocean to feed fresh ocean water into a big pond full of his favorite seafood! He'd managed to find himself one of those French-Vietnamese beauties for his own and married her too.

It felt like begging to think I could offer him anything he wanted. We got to talking though and it turned out he was from Tennessee, which about made us neighbors out here! Talking to him about Kim, I let him know about the promise I'd made, and how much I needed to finish that house.

Well if you can't ask your neighbor for a little help who can you ask, so I dove in and asked him if he had green tin. Just like they said, he did! He didn't get a place like that giving stuff away though. Looking me up and down once, he asked what I could give him for it.

The transportation command was just about a piggy

bank if you were on the inside and that's where I was! I knew the Captain would help me there so I told him I could help with vehicles. He like that all right, and just like that I drove away with a truck load of green tin!

That wasn't the last I saw of Ron Dowell though. He was a man that could make things happen, and we got together back in the states for some adventures too, but I'll have to tell about those some other time. I'll just say he was a man that made things happen WHEREVER he was.

By now I had a considerable stack of lumber, all the tools and nails and hardware I needed, and a green tin roof!

Kim decided I was serious and, tired of waiting her own self, finally agreed to set the date. We were getting married next month! It was getting a little cold at night and she wanted an outdoor ceremony so we had to do it soon.

A couple of weeks later, there I was by the fire again. That fellow had made me a little more alert, something you could be grateful for back then if it didn't kill you first. This time I heard footsteps and looked around.

"Better." was all he said with a little bit of a grin. I was still a little mad about last time so I made some smartass remark like "Anything for you." He sat and we watched the fire for a while.

———

We actually talked a bit that time.
He was definitely American, liked hot dogs, didn't like us being in the war, (we were on the wrong side as far as he was concerned), and said I should call him Cory.

He said "cah" instead of car and such so he was from back east somewhere. You can't really hold where a fellow was born against him though, and two three out four in common wasn't bad.

Never did manage to find out anything about his duty posting, though I got the impression he was a Navy man. Then he left an hour or so later the same way he'd come.

Again, the sentries hadn't seen him come or go when I got around to asking them. I spent some time explaining about our "visitor". I lectured those fellows on guard duty until their ears bled and did some SERIOUS hollering about keeping watch.

They fully understood I was dead ready to have their asses for breakfast if they let him through again. I even put up a reward for whoever spotted him first.

Knowing Cory the little I did, I didn't expect it to do much good. Well, that which doesn't kill us and all that.

I was convinced more than ever that this fellow could stick, shoot, or blow the hell out of anybody he felt like and was for damned sure thrilled as hell I wasn't on his short list.

There was still one thing that bothered me though. Why was a man like that screwing around with our tiny Podunk piece of nothing? I didn't let it bother me too much since my big day was coming!

 Kim put off the wedding date one more week so she could get the right dress. By now I was pretty happy to be put off as long as it was by her.

We were finally married just after my twenty-first birthday in a small but beautiful ceremony in their village Church! Her father gave away the bride and the entire village turned out for the wedding and the celebration after.

Needless to say there was a FINE buffet catered by her parents! That village never saw anything like that before or since and it was good times for a week!

We rode an LCT on a resupply mission to Da Nang for our honeymoon, figuring a cruise was a cruise. My life was as good as it got in Vietnam, but I had one nasty problem.

How on Gods green earth was I going to tell my mama?

Figuring that was something that was just going to have to take care of itself later, I got back down to business. I had a house to build!

 I'd made sure to do every kind of favor I could for the nearest CB's and they came through then. We framed up a pretty nice little three room house inside of

———

two weeks, got the doors and windows on along with some strong shutters for the monsoon, and even had a start on the roof!

Kim and I lived in an extra room at the Orphanage for now. It was a little crowded for newlyweds, but those kids liked having something like a dad around. I have to say I kind of liked it myself.

Not exactly like clockwork, but a few days after I finished the house, I was sitting at the fire again and had to grin when I heard some familiar footsteps. One of the guards, a fellow named Ho I think, start making a racket and came running over with his rifle.

Cory put his hands up just to be on the safe side while I explained to Ho he wasn't getting any reward cause we'd both already be dead if Cory'd wanted us dead. I promised him some extra beer for his effort anyway.

Well I got a nice snappy salute for that which I guess was some consolation anyway. Ho went back to his post and Cory just grinned while I shook my head and swore under my breath.

We got to talking again and I tried steering the conversation around to his duty posting but he wasn't having any. It was just plain odd, but I was still glad for the company since I typically didn't see any Americans for months at a time.

He got real quiet for a minute, then he indicated my boys would be a little more alert if they knew what was coming. His face went grim when I wondered out loud how exactly he knew about that. He gave me a look that wiped the grin off my face and said something that sent a chill up my spine.

"Exactly who's side do you think I'm on?"

Well that took me back a little but I told him I hoped to hell it was mine. He just grinned again and said, "...maybe." Then he pulled out a couple of American issue .45 pistols and handed them to me, explaining he'd "obtained" them during the course of some work he'd been doing recently.

I didn't know what to say to that except "Thank you." These fellows in Song were pretty much woefully under armed and any extra firepower was always welcome. Finding gun belts and holsters for them the next day, I gave one to Loo and put up the other as an extra reward for anybody that could spot Cory on the way in.

Nobody ever did get that other pistol.

During all that time I still had various military duties to perform and I took them even more seriously now that I felt I had Kim to protect as well. I'd taken their old M148 in for a new track before but now the Ontos needed maintenance and I was the man for the job so we radioed up an LCU for the transport. Some of their boys wanted a little R&R in Da Nang so I wound up with a small squad for company.

The LCU grounded on the concrete at Bridge Ramp

___

about 8:00 PM and dropped the gate. Already in the Ontos warming it up, I shoved the sticks forward and it lurched down the ramp and ground up the beach into their compound. The big pile of oil barrels off to the left seemed like a bad place to be so I scooted over to the South side to park it a ways off from those. Wasn't much to do after reporting in to the JG's office so my group and some of those Navy boys got to talking.

About eleven that night a chow truck drove up, and we all grabbed some food and sat in some chairs facing towards the swamp. Most of us sort of leaned back in the chairs against barrels stuffed with dirt they had lining their hootch. The bright painted bands on the Agent Orange barrels added a nice touch of color.

This one fellow got to talking about how he would take apart any VC he met with his bare hands. Apparently he'd had some kind of Karate training and felt like he was ready for them. All I could say to that was "Really? Huh." and just keep on chewing, listening to him talk a pretty good war.

There was vaguely familiar noise, of some kind, from across the swamp, and then a short scream, as a single rocket impacted, across the road, from the West gate, blowing out a pretty good chunk of dirt, and gravel.

Needless to say they'd gotten our attention and we were all on our feet as a full salvo of rockets rose up, flaring into the sky West of us. It looked like that Navy fellow was going to get to test his karate courage in about ten seconds. "INCOMING!!" I yelled and ran off to get behind the Ontos.

175

The first salvo landed in and around the front of the camp without doing much damage, but I figured the next salvo might start hitting stuff that didn't like explosions too much. That's when the deeper throated barking of a couple of fifties started up at the edge of the swamp and tracers came flying through the camp.

 Looking around from behind the tank, I could see those sailors huddled up behind the oil barrels. Swearing and screaming, I managed to convince them to get behind the tank before they got incinerated.

We were all huddled up there when the next salvo hit all around but somehow managed to miss the fuel and ammo. Glancing nervously over at the barrels, by God if it didn't look like there was still somebody there. Now I was a little pissed off 'cause I knew I'd be going to get them.

Rushing across the open ground, I found that loud mouth karate guy on his knees praying. I believe in the power of prayer, so I yelled "AMEN!" and grabbed him by the arm.

"ON YOUR FEET NOW!", I insisted. He didn't need much prodding and we managed to get behind the tank pretty quick, tracers flying around us and spanking the armor. A couple of salvos later, a rocket hit and that oil went off like Napalm. The heat from the blast about burned the hair off all of us.

It didn't look or sound like there was any kind of defensive action being taken. When I asked the sailors at the tank about it they indicated this was the first time they'd come under fire. Waiting for what seemed like a lull in the rockets, I crouched and ran over to the JG's office to find out what the plan was. I was swimming upstream through a bunch of Navy boys to get there too. It looked like they were bugging out to the boats. Seemed pretty sensible to me.

I ran into him on the way out with a box full of papers and bottles of Old Crow. Grabbing him by the arm I shouted above the noise, "So what's the plan sir?!" He looked at me for a second, seeming a little bewildered and asked, "Do you think we ought to...", we both hit the ground for a bit while another salvo of rockets played itself out,"...ought to put up a white flag?!?", he finished. Now the thought of hiking about a quarter mile through the swamp and jungle to the launch site with a white flag would have been pretty funny if we weren't about to die.

"Hard to surrender to a rocket Sir!" I yelled, "I think they've got a couple of fifties running at the edge of the swamp you might try to hike out to, but I wouldn't recommend it!!" That seemed to take the steam out of his idea and he took off toward the boats.

Finally hearing some return, I decided to get a piece of that before we got overrun. The boats started looking even better to me as another salvo of rockets hit with shrapnel rattling all over, every hit digging out about a ten foot hole.

Stepping out of the buildings, there was an Army Private unloading an M-16 into the muzzle flash of the

177

VC fifties. I decided to follow his fine example since there wasn't much to do about the rockets. I wasn't sure where the rest of my squad was, but knowing those boys I'd bet they were doing the same.

Grabbing my rifle and some clips from the Ontos, I ran forward to help set up crossfire. It turned out there wasn't any good hard cover, but it was well lit! Rather large bullets started hitting around me and my hands were shaking so bad I had to crouch and use my knee to shove a clip into the gun.

That's when I noticed what looked like a big invisible dog digging at the ground next to my right boot. It seemed like forever but was really only about half a second before I realized that one of those fifties must be sighted a little low and to the left, AND that my idea was an extremely bad one. Picking up one boot and then the other, I almost started dancing then realized there was a better option.

It looked like all the machine gun fire was coming from two locations pretty close together in the jungle about west of the compound. It was time for "The Pig".

Running back to the Ontos, I'd got just about in it, when a shockwave threw me and a wall of dirt up against the sloped front armor. The newly loosened dirt met my grimacing mouth as I rolled off. Vietnam didn't taste too bad as it turns out.

My leg didn't feel right and my head hurt. That karate fellow pulled me behind the tank as another salvo hit,

"YOU'RE BLEEDING!" he yelled, pushing a rag to my head. I put my hand to my forehead and it came away red.

I was flat mad now.

Shaking it off best I could, I climbed into the drivers hatch; I started 'er up. Those boys hollered at me since they were losing their cover and I surely didn't look like I should be driving any heavy machinery. "YOU MIGHT WANT TO CONSIDER THOSE BOATS! RECKON I'LL BE THERE MYSELF SHORTLY!" I hollered back, ramming the sticks forward then hauling back on the right one to get it turned toward the front gate.

What I had remembered was we ALWAYS kept that thing loaded 'cause you never knew what might happen.

The tank busted through the gate and I got it pointed at the muzzle flash. Stomping out tracers like a base drum, I adjusted a little with the sticks.

Fifties splattered on the inch thick front armor just under the drivers hatch, showering my face with fine metal shards. I doubled up inside the tank with my palm pressed to my left eye for a second, then stretching and bellowing out my pain and anger, I slapped behind me at the fire control panel trying to hit any button I could.

Reckon I hit the right one.

The roar was deafening as all six guns fired, and all eight tons jumped off the ground, bucking me out of the seat. The back blast annihilated everything behind for about thirty feet, and the jungle at the swamps edge must have just disintegrated for a about a hundred yard front as thousands of heavy steel darts chewed it up.

Those VC had either joined the choir or decided my Pig beat their pajamas any day of the week 'cause bullets stopped bouncing off the tank. By the time I managed to get my head back out the hatch that Private was standing beside the right track, whooping up a storm and laughing his head off as he pumped more bullets into the Jungle.

Looking around we realized the place was pretty much all ours. The next salvo of rockets landed behind us and we decided pretty much simultaneously we didn't want it.

I cranked it around while he jumped in the commanders hatch. We closed up and tracked back down to the beach where the rest of the Navy personnel were loading onto the last LCU. "THAT WAS AMAZING!!", he congratulated me above the noise of the engine and the rockets, laughing and pounding me on the back.

"YEAH THIS IS ONE NASTY SUMBITCH!", I had to agree.

We made it to the beach, rocket shrapnel pinging off the outside as the tank bounced through the blasts. Pulling up next to the LCU, I popped out and spotted a

Chief Petty Officer.

"IS IT TIME TO GO?!", I demanded.

"YOU CAN'T PARK THAT DAMN THING ON MY
SHIP!" he roared back at me, "IT'LL BE ANOTHER
TEN BEFORE THIS GUTLESS WONDER STARTS
ANYWAY!!"

Turned out the JG had left with a bunch of boys on
"the good" LCU and left a pig of an LCU that was
taking a long time to get warmed up. We were stuck
here until it did.

There was no use waiting around for a rocket to hit,
and I was so pumped up and pissed off at that JG
anyway, I had to do something. When I asked the
Private about participating in a combat recovery
mission he grinned and saluted with a "YES SIR!" We
buttoned up again and ran the tank back to the JG's
office through the rockets where I got every bottle of
good whiskey I could find, not sure what the Private
was partial to, if anything.

Trying to figure out the best way to get it out of there I
realized I'd found the perfect reload for the Ontos.
Dumping out the shells from all six guns I filled them
with every bottle of Jack Daniels, Old Crow and
whatever else I could find. Wasn't much of a hard
drinking man myself, but I knew Captain Cong had to
sell things on the black market to pay his men and this
would be a Godsend.

We were a good thirty minutes into it by now and the

rockets weren't letting up. As soon as they got the other LCU started I left the Ontos out on the beach and high tailed it out to sea with the rest of them where we sat and watched the show until three in the morning. We were pretty lucky the LCU didn't get hit before that. It wasn't for lack of rockets, that's for sure.

I heard later those Navy boys that hid behind the tank got medals for defending the camp. Knowing what it could be like your first time under fire, and all the crazy things that happened over there, the best way to describe how I feel about that is "Good for them!" Everybody that got shot at by the VC over there deserved a medal as far as I'm concerned.

The next day I went about my business with the transportation command moving some parts around while I waited on the Ontos to get another track. The day after my boys started telling me I'd better get to a medic 'cause my leg was swelling up. I told them we had more important things to do but the truth was I was scared to DEATH of NEEDLES.

Well later that day, the leg had swollen up, bigger than my head and I just plain old fell over. When I woke up, at China Beach, I had a needle in my arm, and a doctor, on my wrist, telling me how lucky I, was to be alive.

I tell you what; I was all about hospitals after that. If one of my boys got a paper cut I'd take them in. After all we had the best health care in Vietnam; even the VC would come to us instead of their own. Theirs was about as likely to kill as cure.

Seemed like there was always something odd happening when I brought in a tank for maintenance.

Like the one time when I was waiting on a replacement track for the M-48 when a couple of officers came into the hootch and just pointed at a few of us. "You, you, you, and you, come with us."

No mention what they wanted or where we were going. They drove us out to some kind of half-assed shooting range near the hills and trained us on pump shotguns while half a dozen or so snipers scanned the hill side with their scopes.

I wasn't sure if they needed to fill some kind of requirement or were using us for sniper bait. I suppose it could've been both, but that kind of efficiency wasn't the military I'd come to know and love.

Sometimes I'd be volunteered for some kind of duty station when I was there for a while.

Once I was volunteered for MP Sergeant of the watch for a few days on part of the Airbase there at DaNang. We got a report of a noisy party getting violent on a balcony at one of the clubs there. Checking out some weapons, me and a six man patrol went to check it out, approaching them from the cover of some buildings.

   It was about as raucous as it got there with half to mostly naked women, booze, and a couple of bodies in the mud in front of the balcony. They looked more

———

like they'd jumped than been pushed cause one of them
was laughing and the other was still breathing.
The loudest, rowdiest, most obnoxious folks on that
balcony were a few black fellows that looked like they
really had a head of steam on. Now I'm not saying
what you think, that would have been white boys any
other day of the week. It just depends on whose got
their steam on that day.

In this case though it was definitely some black fellows
leading the pack. The boys with me were all white and
a couple of them seemed to have some kind of lynch
mob background 'cause they wanted to just open fire
and KILL ALL of them!

The other fellows weren't necessarily against that
'cause they'd sent a few MP's home in boxes on
account of just this kind of activity. From my little bit
of time in Okinawa I knew what they meant.

Well, being who I was, I was strictly against murdering
U.S. military personnel of any color or service branch.
We about, and I kid you not, had our own firefight
about it right there on the street. Thank God, and my
grandpa, and I had some time at the pulpit. I drew on
every trick I knew and some of Grandpa's, to finally
convince them, to let me go talk to those boys first.

Getting up to that balcony, I got right up in the face of
the worst fellow there and explained the situation in
my best southern drawl so he'd know I was serious.

He gave me a "Say what?" so I gave it to him one more
time, explaining that I knew for a fact if they didn't

straighten up when I asked my boys they would open fire, if I wanted them to, or not. They might not even care too much, if I bought it in the process, so please would they stand down, since I didn't want to die any more than they did.

Looking where I pointed he could see some muzzles aiming up at us and still had some good sense drunk or not. Turning about two shades paler to light brown, he started slapping and yelling at the fellows around him to shut up. Him being the ring leader and all...they did.

They'd done their part so I hollered at my patrol to stand down and was pretty relieved when they actually did. I'd still half expected to have died up there with a fairly serious case of lead poisoning no matter what happened.

That was another nice thing about Song, those boys had a little respect for me at least 'cause Captain Cong did.

I don't remember if I said any kind of prayers that night, but you can be for sure there was a thank you in there if I did.

Every man in the village all knew the VC were there because we encountered them on patrols. I wasn't often risked on those because of my place there as the attaché. After a few months though, married or not, Captain Cong decided it was time.

It was a long range patrol with nine Vietnamese boys that was supposed to last about a week. They weren't big corn fed fellows, but they were wiry as well as highly motivated, excellent, and merciless fighters. Along with our standard ordinance, we carried an m-60, a couple of launchers, a small mortar, plenty of ammo and grenades, and nice sharp combat knives. We were definitely what you'd call armed to the teeth.

Knowing what might await the people in Song made it easy for me to kill VC on patrol. The nice thing about being with a unit of South Vietnamese is they weren't subject to rules of engagement that crippled all the American forces in Vietnam. If we ran into trouble we just got the job done.

The Captain sent his best man, a fellow named Loo, Lieutenant Loo. Their uniforms were perfect for the jungle with their tiger striped camouflage. I'd gotten one almost as soon as I'd arrived so I made good use of it now.

Having talked with the leaders of their patrols that returned, I knew where we were most likely to find them. I had a terrain map that I'd marked with all the known trails and highlighted the ones they seemed to use the most. It was my first long range patrols in this area so I discussed it with Loo and listened carefully to his advice. We decided to proceed toward a particularly ideal location for an Ambush and see if we could do some damage.

We started on the next dry day we had. Threading our way through the small winding levies that separated the green rice patties. Being from a small farm myself, it was just one more thing I loved about this place.

186

As a boy I'd spent as much time as I could run around the woods so the jungle was always deceptively peaceful and beautiful to me. I'd seen blood dripping off the leaves, and entrails wrapped around trees before though, so I was definitely what you'd have to call vigilant in spite of that. When Loo took point I marched slack and watched him carefully to learn what I could.

We made it to the ambush site without incident. Loo checked the trail and indicated recent activity so we had a right to expect more company in a day or so. In spite of that we setup the ambush as quickly as possible just in case.

We sat there for two days and our patience was rewarded when what looked like a full VC squad twelve strong came into sight. Loo was beside me on the mM-60 and I had a launcher ready with an m-16 beside me. The rest of our squad of eight was on the opposite side of the trail with a direct line of fire down the wide bend they were coming up to our location on.

They had pretty much nowhere to go when we opened up. Five of them died immediately and we chewed into the rest from concealed hard cover while they tried desperately to find a little ridge of dirt to put between us. I was pumping grenades into the concealment a few had managed to find. It didn't do them any good since I knew they were there, and I heard them scream as the shrapnel bit into them. They'd all be dead shortly.

I had trained these men in the tactics and philosophy of the United States Marines the best way I knew how, the way I was trained. It was starting to look like I'd done a good job. The Marine Corps had taught me, and I'd taught these men that you live by the squad, you die by the squad, the squad is your life, and you don't leave a man behind.

What happened when the Jungle exploded around us was eight highly trained grown men went eight different directions at top speed, and didn't look back.

There must have been another fifty to a hundred AKs, a machine gun or two and at least one RPG that opened up on us from behind our intended victims through the foliage. This squad seemed to have been the lead element of about a full company, and they definitely seemed none to happy about our mistreatment of their comrades.

As the commanding officer, trying to hold it together enough for an orderly retreat, I looked over at Loo to order him to fall back. The m-60 was there but he was just gone.

We had set up excellent lines of retreat and he knew better than to hang around. I knew if he'd gone that he was following the others. VC were streaming past my position on the opposite side of the trail pursuing the part of our ambush they'd seen and were between me and the village already.

I was left with one unbelievably bad choice.

188

One of them must have seen me because a hail of bullets followed me into the underbrush. I tell you what son, those fellows in the Olympics are fast, but a skinny short white boy in combat boots could beat them any day of the week with a bakers dozen of AKs trying to chew up his ass. I did my level best to make sure they didn't get much of a shot at that either.

Grabbing my M-16, I flat ran straight into that jungle, directly away from the village, away from safety, away from my beautiful young wife, away from all the warmth and light in the world as far as I knew.

I was on my own now.

Seemed like a good idea not to stop until Cambodia, but then they were all up in there too. I paused to get my bearings but just a little later the underbrush was rustling as a group of men came up behind me. It could've been mine but that would've been more luck. They were coming up pretty slowly and I didn't know why, but I took advantage of that to get ahead of them.

Immediately deciding not to do anything to make these boys want my hide any worse, I decided to just throw them off where I could. I'd left the launcher but had the 40mm grenades. Grenade bandoliers and vests weren't easy to come by so it was pretty common for the grenades to be carried loose and get lost. That could be an advantage.

Moving forward as quickly and quietly as possible, I found a stream and turned down it, stirring up the muck until I found an overhanging tree. I tossed a couple of the small grenades downstream about twenty feet or so, jumped that branch to the bank, continued into the jungle about fifty feet, then went quietly back upstream. The hope being that anybody behind me would follow the silt downstream, pick up the grenades, and continue following the water until they hit the sea. A fellow could dream after all.

Stopping for a moment behind a stand of bamboo, I waited and listened. Knowing Vietnamese was valuable, but not always comforting. I could hear enough as they continued down stream to tell there was a twelve man squad of NVA following me, they'd seen I was white and suspected I was an officer and American advisor, and I'd killed a few of their personal friends. Chuck wanted me WORSE than DEAD in a bad way and I was in some real trouble.

Waiting in cover, after about half an hour I heard them come back upstream. I was facing a fellow that had done a little hunting. I'd been hunting most of my life and followed around some pretty cagey critters. Follow a couple of hounds after a raccoon for a while and you'll know what I mean. Now I was the coon and they were the hunters but it turned out they only had one good hound.

Getting treed by him was what I had to avoid.

I'm not sure why they didn't come out where the tree hung over the stream, I guess being even shorter than me and not having any kind of jump shot it didn't occur to them, but they hadn't been fooled by the grenades. They thought I was just backtracking, but that kind of luck couldn't be counted on again. I needed a place to hide and a real plan if I was going to get out of this alive.

I took advantage of their mistake after they'd passed, leaping into the water and heading downstream. Finding a fork with a tiny tributary and heading up it, I found what I was after, a thicket of trees surrounded with dense foliage all the way to the waters edge.

Continuing upstream for a while, I found another overhanging branch. Making more tracks upstream, I tossed another 40mm grenade as far as I could up it, then backtracked to the branch. Climbing out on it, I made sure to leave a bunch of mud and marks, then ran a couple of big circles back to it.

Backtracking downstream to the thicket, I made my way very carefully up the bank and into the thickest part of the tree's and underbrush, waiting for them to pass me again. I felt sure this fellow would track me up in here and catch my false trail long enough for me to get another good head start.

Anyway, even if they took a while picking up my new trail, it would be completely dark soon and this was a good place to rest. There's no way they'd track me in the dark. It was almost always absolutely black in the jungle at night. I mean like you can't see your hand if you wave it in front of your face, dark like a coal mine at night during an eclipse. No time to be running around and they'd be stopping soon too.

Waiting, listening until long after dark, as I faded off to sleep the reason for their slow pursuit became obvious. Chuck knew Marine training too and must think the squad had regrouped and I was with them.

We had succeeded in putting the fear of God into them and they were moving slowly to avoid dying. I'd caught a badly needed break. Hope that the rest of the squad had survived, of returning to Song and my wife, filled me as I faded off to a light and fitful sleep with my pistol in one hand, and my head resting on the butt of my rifle.

They thought I had a plan.

Waking in the early light to the sound of men moving slowly up the nearby stream, it was time to start moving again. Listening for a moment I could tell this was the same squad from yesterday, but they were jawing about "comrade sergeant" so and so going this direction and "comrade Lieutenant" going some other, so I learned a good chunk of that company was hunting "us".

I had to smile at that, but then the thought of just me facing all of them sobered me up pretty quick. Deciding to work my way downstream to a nearby river, I slithered carefully off through the underbrush, not daring to get back in the streams again.

Different squads kept popping up all day so progress was slow, never getting more than a hundred yards before stopping again, sometimes for hours. Eaten alive by insects, I covered myself with mud the best I could to keep them off and give me better cover.

For two days I stayed flat in the underbrush, not even daring to sit up half the time. They got as close as twenty feet and the second night a squad camped within thirty feet of me and I listened to them joke and talk until they fell asleep.

The next day, finally making it to the big water, I slid into the current and started working my way downriver, and then stopped. I'm not sure how to explain it, it just felt wrong, and the further I went the worse it felt. Suddenly I heard a familiar voice in my head, small and quiet but undeniable.

"Turn."

It was frustrating as hell. Finally on my way back to the coast I had to turn away from home again, but I knew it was the right thing to do so I went. Crawling out at night to dry off and rest and then back into the river the next day. The third evening of that I started to pull out on the bank and heard a group of men coming toward me.

Quickly pushing into some nearby reeds, I watched as another VC squad came to the rivers edge to rest. Several fellows were washing their feet while some smoked. These weren't any of the ones I'd heard before. A couple of them even went swimming.

Then their Sergeant announced they were sleeping here.

The obvious place for them to set up camp was in the cover next to the reeds I was in. Working quickly to cut the biggest reed I could find, I slid underwater to try breathing through it, while they started setting up their camp behind the cover of the reeds.

Well I guess it works for some people, and Loo had sworn up and down it worked when he showed me how, but that damned reed wasn't worth spit to me. All I could do now was pray they didn't decide to mess around in the reeds, and hope a snake didn't get me. They had some pretty big ones over there and it just made sense they wouldn't pass up a warm meal already half drowned. Out of rations by then, I was getting pretty hungry myself so I could sympathize, just not enough to put away my knife.

There wasn't much in the way of sleep that night, but I gave up worrying after a few hours and actually began to enjoy the water. Sitting still and just floating, completely surrounded by warm water, disconnected from the world, was a nice change. If it hadn't been for the constant threat of getting blown to hell I'm sure it would have been pretty damned cathartic, or maybe that's why it felt so good.

Couldn't rightly say, but it did seem strange to be anything but scared spitless with Anacondas in the water, and imminent painful death just sawing away twenty feet from my nose. I suppose there's a point where it just isn't any good worrying. You had to give it up or get a permanent full-time position being touched in the head.

My momma was always saying to me and my dad, "You boys just worry me to death!" One thing was for sure, after that night, there wasn't much on this planet that would worry me unnecessarily for more than a few hours. I figured I'd have to recommend this to mama the next time she mentioned that to me.

Surfacing occasionally to listen to them, and then for a while in the morning darkness, I saw them stirring just about dawn and ducked slowly back under for as long as I could whenever the got near. They moved around for a bit and one fellow must have gotten closer than ten feet since I could make out a vague figure against the light. I had a grenade in my fist the whole time he was moving around, washing a dish or something. My preference was to blow us all to HELL rather than go with THESE old boys.

Fortunately, it didn't come to that, and they moved off.

Charming as my waterbed had been, I decided to take a day off out of the water. There was some good thick cover nearby for drying out and a few hours nap. A good bit of day was left when I woke, so I cleaned my guns the best I could manage and started hiking overland, keeping the river in my hearing distance and trying to make sure to stay the hell out of anybody else's. That night I slept dry for the first time in over a week.

Mostly in the water during the day, on land at night, for about another week that continued. Eating whatever I could find at that point, the snakes and bugs around there must have thought it was Sherman

———
195

marching through Georgia. When it felt like I'd gone far enough upriver, I turned North toward the DMZ overland.

If there was anything bigger than a bald faced monkey between me and the DMZ I didn't see or hear it on the way North. Moving pretty carefully though, it still took me another week to get there. It was easy to tell when I'd arrived because my fellow countrymen opened FIRE on me.

Fortunately, I'd arrived during the day, starting across the cleared fire zone waving at them and hallooing when suddenly they put some across my bow, presumably to get my attention, which it definitely did. I got myself behind the biggest tree I could find, and they chewed in to it. I hollered my lungs out until the bullets stopped bouncing around me. "THIS IS SARGEANT JOHN ROBERT MIZELL USMC, CEASE FIRE, CEASE FIRE!!"

"COME OUT IN THE OPEN, NOW!", they ordered. Needless to say I complied, stepping out into the open where I could see two M-16s and a fifty trained on me. They let me into the line but kept a gun on me until they'd gotten on the radio and verified some of my story. Expecting an apology when they got off the horn, they said "What exactly the hells were you doing out there?!"

I was home...I guess.

They seemed more annoyed they'd wasted bullets on me than grateful I wasn't dead. Looking at the wide variety of firepower in and around their bunker, I became grateful I hadn't tried coming through at night, imagining it wouldn't have gone so well.

They did let me radio ahead though, and I requested a message forwarded to the Captain that I was alright. There were supply trucks that ran up and down the DMZ, and as soon as I could get on one of those going toward the coast I did, then worked my way down Highway One back to song.

It turned out the rest of the squad had a few problems, but had still gotten back a couple of weeks before me. Unbelievably, they were all ALIVE!

We slapped each other on the back and laughed out loud, happy to see each other and disbelieving our amazing good fortune, thanking God a number of times out loud. They went silent then, looking behind me.

Turning to look, there was Kim.

Before I could take a breath she was in my arms, crying and kissing me, taking all the love I could show in front of these soldiers as her due. She never thought I was dead and told me right there it was one of the reasons she'd married me. She knew I'd always come back.

At that moment I knew it was time to tell mama about her. It was time to tell her who I was going to be coming home to the rest of my life. I started a letter that night, deciding I'd send it home with some of my

---

things in case I didn't make it.

The more I thought about it though, the more I knew I had to have Kim with me when I told her. If she could just SEE her, talk to her, and know what a wonderful person she was mama would just have to love her almost as much as I did. How could she not?

After the Captain heard my story, he decided not to risk me on any long range patrols any more.

It was getting into the real dead of winter by now and it was time for more maintenance on the armor so we called up a boat and got it loaded up. Well I guess Cory had gotten word from Kim where I was 'cause he drove up in a Jeep with what looked like a couple of Vietnamese officers and asked me to go for a ride over to the BX!

If I was a little surprised at his nerve, I was still dying with curiosity. Since I hadn't been assigned any other temporary duties yet...I went.

We went in and those two officers kept pointing at stuff and asking me to buy it for them. Looking over at Cory he'd just shake his head so I'd make some kind of excuse.

For some reason those two wanted to get over to the deep water pier then. A couple of MP's stopped us as we pulled up and I figured that whatever jig we were doing was entirely UP.

Well I saw a whole new side of Cory then. He did some slick talking on those fellows and would every now and then throw a question at me and I'd just say "Yes sir." Well I guess with all those lieutenant bars in the car and a story that for all I knew was true, we managed to get onto the pier.

They had us pull up to a ship there and they started radioing somebody on board. Then before you know it we were on the ship. Friend or not, he was starting to make me a little nervous by now but we just played cards for awhile then left.

After that it was dinner at what seemed to be the house of one of the Officers mother. I tell you what she could have given a lesson or two to Kim on Vietnamese food.

After that we dropped those two off at the Transportation Command, and then he started over to China Beach saying there was some kind of party going on.

Now it WAS plenty cold by then but they'd got a big tent heated up so you'd sweat bullets and they had the coldest beer I'd ever tasted in Vietnam that was a big piece of the reason. There were huge Ice filled coolers of it and I drank until I couldn't see the cans, waking up at my hootch without even knowing how I got there.

I'm still trying to figure out what that was all about sometimes and was actually hoping maybe somebody out there could tell me.

Next time I was in Hue a couple of official looking fellows looked me up and sat me down. They had a picture they wanted me to identify and it was Cory.

These two had the same look in their eyes that Cory did and I knew I was sitting with a couple of fellows who had a little less respect for life than most folks I knew even in the Marine Corp, even in Vietnam.

Still, I didn't see any point in lying about knowing him, figuring they were asking me because they'd been pointed my way. Fortunately they didn't think I knew as much as I did so when I dove off into a purposely meandering southern fried story about him wondering around my camp they chalked it all up to ignorance and left.

At least I hoped they did. The one thing definitely worse than having a man like Cory wanting to skin you alive (and I mean that) is having two just like him wanting the same.

Cory showed up at Song a week or two later around dinner time. I wasn't sure if I should tell him about those two that'd shown me his picture. I pretty much wear my heart on my sleeve and all I could manage with my plate was playing around with the rice so he knew something was up.

He looked grim for a second then asked, "Has anybody been asking about me Bob?" Well I just COULDN'T out and out tell him 'cause I just couldn't bring myself to work against my own people, but I suggested there were some fellows who knew he came here sometimes and he might want to extremely careful.

Describing one of those fellows to a tee, he asked if that was one of the men I'd talked to. I nodded, knowing we both knew what was after him now. He stiffened up for a second and was clearly agitated. "Yeah I know that guy.", he finished.

Kim looked back and forth at both of us, a little bewildered.

Nodding thoughtfully for a second then he fixed me with a stare and added, "Is that all they know Bob?" I looked him right in the eye and said "Yes sir."

He held my gaze for a second, nodding a little, then sat back in his seat running a hand through his hair again. "Well," he sighed heavily;"...that's not good news." I just nodded.

We sat for a minute.

"Well...I reckon we won't be seeing you for a while.", I finally ventured.

He just nodded.

"Well Bob, Kim," he finished, wiping his mouth,"...thanks for dinner. Thanks for everything. I better get going."

Kim hadn't ever known any of my friends except for

Cory, so she gave him a little hug before he left.

The Captain had me go into Hue on some business for the transportation command about a week later. Just like always the Marine Corp managed to get a hold of me and shipped me off to do some night watches at the Airbase in Da Nang. I made sure to get a message to the Captain, knowing he'd let Kim know what was happening.

There were any number of rowdy parties and it was part of my job to keep things from getting out of hand, so I and the biggest fellows I could find went around making sure to be seen.

Spotting one of those fellows that'd asked about Cory, I worked my way over to him, tapping him on the shoulder. I could tell he recognized me when he turned around so I went on and asked him if he'd ever found that fellow he asked me about, smiling like I didn't care.

He looked right through me for a second then just said, "Yeah, we found him.", and walked away, leaving me with that stupid smile carved on my face as my heart sank. Well now I knew what that meant for Cory. He was dead as a rock. All I could hope was that he'd died easy.

The Phoenix program was not something I'd heard of until after the war. I'd swear on a stack of Bibles that fellow was in it though. Look it up and you'll see what I mean. I knew Cory had gone over the line and what help from a man like that to the VC could mean for

little villages like mine, but I knew he was my friend.
Now he was as dead as you could get.
It wasn't just hard to tell who the VC were, now it was
getting difficult to tell who my friends were.

The upcoming Tet holiday put all the South
Vietnamese I knew into a pretty good mood. Even
Captain Cong was ready for the celebration. He
gathered up his officers including Lieutenant Loo and
myself, and drove us all into Hue for coffee at his
favorite shop on the first day of the celebration.

Sitting next to a front window in the shop, we had a
great view of what passed for a quaint street in Hue,
and the coffee was excellent. Turned out to be a good
thing it was on the second floor too.

  Hearing gunfire that morning wasn't terribly
alarming, like I said before, everybody had guns.
When Captain Cong jumped out of his chair and yelled
"Oh shit!" in English however, we all got with the
program.

Outside the window were VC running past with
bayonets fixed. Not the garden variety farm hands
either, these boys were wearing NVA uniforms and
moving like trained soldiers.

The area we were in had been overrun. The main push
of the Tet offensive had taken us completely by
surprise.

We got the hell out of there as fast as we could, taking
the jeep through every short cut and whore lined back

alley we could find. Explosions and firefights seemed to be all around us. We gradually left them behind and high tailed it back to the village where we immediately put everybody on high alert.

My call sign was Calcutta golf five. They made it long and about impossible to pronounce properly for anybody, but a native English speaker so the VC would have a hard time messing up communications. Since I spoke both Vietnamese and English, it seemed like I got a pretty good picture of the fighting from the radio traffic.

We heard calls for dust offs, reinforcements, artillery and tank fire control, air strikes, and more. It sounded like they even had a few Ontos rolling around in there. I tell you what; you could pretty fairly say it was tense for a number of days. Everybody was either in a foxhole watching the perimeter, or in a bunker glued to the radio, until we collapsed from exhaustion.

It wasn't all happening in Hue and Da Nang though. We got hit during those two weeks with what seemed like probing attacks. Mainly small arms fire and mortars. There were any number of VC that we caught fixing to get in through the wire, but they failed every time.

We'd catch one at it and holler at him to surrender, but they'd just charge or pull out a grenade and we were forced to give open fire or get one in the face ourselves. That's just the way it was. We defended ourselves and buried them with a fair amount of dignity. I sincerely doubt they'd have returned the favor.

We didn't just ask them to surrender out of the kindness of our hearts either. American forces paid the South Vietnamese for every prisoner they handed over for interrogation. The VC had been told any number of lies about the horrors awaiting anyone falling into our hands. I can say it was just about a complete lie concerning our forces and only partial truth even if they fell into the hands of the somewhat less kindly South Vietnamese.

Lyndon Johnson got on the armed forces radio network and assured all of Vietnam that we would never leave them. I knew for sure I wasn't going to leave, not without Kim. We were both leaving standing up or I was going in a box as far as I was concerned.

While all the main population centers had been hit on or around the Tet holiday, for weeks afterward there were reports of outlying villages and small towns getting decimated in what seemed like related operations. They were nasty too, wiping out everybody or close to it. I figure they were trying to get some back for their failures in Hue.

Hearing about that panicked me and I laid on the entire extra defense I could get a hold of. Packing in extra claymores and razor wire, and then crowning it with another fifty, so we had enough now to create crossfire anywhere on the perimeter.

I didn't know if we were ready or not, but I'd done

everything I could. All we could do now was put on extra guards and wait for it.

Another month passed before anything serious happened. We'd stood down from the alert and been that way for at least a few weeks. Things had pretty much returned to normal.

We didn't see them coming at all.

Our long and short range patrols all came back unmolested. They must have watched us go by, given orders to stay out of our way. It's not too hard in the jungle.

The day even started peacefully enough, the calm lasting until just after dinner. Kim had gone to the orphanage and I was walking around the perimeter, watching the jungle for any sign of activity. I was nervous for some reason, pacing like a caged lion. It put the men on edge too.

Then the rockets started screaming, mortars came pounding in, tracers came flying through, and all hell generally broke loose. There had to have been somebody in the town helping them because the first couple of salvos were right on the money, taking out the radio tower and hitting the Captains house.

There were only about forty fighting men among us altogether and I'd say maybe two companies is what started coming at us from every piece of jungle I could see. They had to come in over at least a thousand feet of open ground though, and we made them pay for every inch. Dozens of poppy red spots bloomed in the

rice patties where they dropped. Then the M-48 and
the Ontos started singing base. The whole choir was in
tune and the saints were marching in, but there were so
many of them.

I'd seen a man throw a live chicken in water full of
alligators once. They'd hit our main radio and the
Captain was probably dead already. All I had was a
hand radio, my M16, and with those kind of numbers
coming at us...about half a prayer. I got my ass on that
radio and started demanding the choppers that Colonel
from White Elephant had promised, figuring I'd better
come up with something better than that chicken did,
and in less time.

There was no answer.

Then the wire started singing as they closed on our
perimeter and stormed the compound. Our claymores
were exploding in their faces and the fifty crossfire
was harvesting whole squads, but they kept coming
like it was confetti, jumping over the razor wire on the
bodies of their own dead. I'd never seen men so
anxious to get on with dying.

We were outnumbered at least three to one. I unloaded
a clip into that boiling mess and saw a number of VC
fall.

We began retreating, some toward the beach to make
an escape in the few boats we had, some to the
orphanage to make a stand there. Soldiers retreating to
the beach were cut down in short order by the VC that
had landed in their own boats.

They were coming in from the water as well. I'm sure that was supposed to have happened first to get our attention before the main thrust from the jungle. Good to know Murphy worked for the VC too.

By then it was just about every man for himself and nobody knew which way to turn.

Then I saw Kim in the doorway to the orphanage with a couple of the little ones. She was waving at me, desperation and fear alternately coursing across her face as the children clung to her legs.

Loo and I locked eyes for a moment and we saw the end in each others gaze. He yelled at me to go to her, but I was already gone. It didn't seem fast enough. Loo's loud orders seemed so far away.

Then the children suddenly seemed calm, bowing their heads. Kim stretched her hand out to me as the wind tousled her hair. She was yelling something I couldn't hear, maybe my name. It all twisted and distorted as grenades and bullets seemed to play the strings of time. I'd felt it before but it seemed unfamiliar and wrong now too.

There were just so many of them.

Her eye's. I remember her eye's just before the mortar hit, about ten feet away from them. She knew, I'd come back. She'd always known. Coming a few feet toward me, Kim was slapped back through the air into the door frame, and the children were knocked over.

The white paint around the entryway was suddenly speckled red.

Oh God, Jesus, God no! I was next to her then. Watching the blood pour out of her head. Throwing away my rifle, I held her in my arms, feeling the life draining out of her. It had been a little boy and girl with her. They were so still now. Cradling Kim in my arms, I guess to protect what was left of her from whatever else might happen, I closed my eyes, ready to go with them.

I heard the shouts of desperate men about to breath their last. Loo's orders were suddenly cut short.

Then I heard another rocket. That was just crazy, why would they be firing rockets now at their own men? It had a different sound and it occurred to me it was going to hit pretty close about the same split second it did. A single piece of metal exploded into the inside of my left knee and spun me around, throwing Kim out of my embrace.

Roaring in agony, pushing at the ground with my arms, I opened my eyes one last time. The little girl was there on the ground next to me, her fingers trembled slightly. Then something hit me in the back of the head and this world was gone.

I heard they came a few hours later. They'd never gotten my radio calls. Maybe the VC were jamming us. Maybe the batteries had died. Maybe something else. By the time I had a chance to think about it, it didn't matter anymore.

———

The report indicated the attack had been so intense that they'd heard it all the way to Hue. That's why the choppers had finally come. All they found were bodies.

Still, they decided to dig around for what was left of me, finding me under a piece of roof that had blown off the orphanage, bloody and broken up. Pulling me out, they stuck me on the Chopper to ship home.

Never leave a man behind.

The way I heard it, they had me about halfway in a body bag and in the air when they noticed I was still warm, then that I was breathing. Being pretty messed up, they took me directly to China beach.

At China Beach they declared me too broken for them to fix but got me stabilized. I was still unconscious when they put me on a plane to Balboa Hospital in San Diego.

That's where I had been for two months when my eyes finally opened, and everything I had known was gone.

It was hard even to speak at first. When I got enough voice back I demanded to know what had happened. The doctor gave a clinically precise explanation of my injuries. Shrapnel had shattered my left knee and a bullet had made a crease in the back of my skull. There were some broken bones from the building falling on me too. He wasn't sure if I'd walk again.

"No!", I insisted, "I want to know what happened to

The Village!" He didn't know, but I kept pushing and a week or so later a Gunnery Sergeant showed up with a folder that contained the report on that action and my rescue. I hadn't gotten any new glasses yet so I asked him to read it to me.

There wasn't much to mark the passing of my world. They hadn't found anybody alive but me. The viciousness of the VC had been sudden and complete. Men, women, and children, all dead. The buildings were all burning when they'd got there.

There'd been no VC bodies. That was the surest sign of complete victory for them since they liked to haul off all their dead even more than us. It was some kind of a religious thing with them.

 The report noted there were signs of VC casualties out in the surrounding rice patties where they couldn't clean the blood out of the water. I made sure that Gunny knew we'd raised the price on our real estate. That was the least I could do for my men. They'd fought as well as anybody could. We all did.

After the lights went out that night, I let myself cry. When I fell asleep, I saw Kim in my dreams, reliving those last terrible minutes over and over. In those nightmares I kept trying to stop the blood, but it kept coming out between my fingers, past bandages, soaking my clothes until I woke up yelling, tangled in the white sheets and traction lines.

You could hear something like that happening every night in that ward. I suppose there must have been about twenty four broken up men in there. Something like what happened to me or worse was relived by somebody in there about every evening. Any given night the sounds of muffled crying drifted from somewhere else in the room.

After a few days, drugs were all that would get me asleep. It was deep dreamless sleep too. I guess the mind won't let you torture yourself in the world of dreams if you can't wake up and stop it. That's the way it was while I was in a coma too, a desperately needed mercy I can say.

Kim was dead and Song was gone.. just gone.

They said I might not walk again. I wasn't sure what to think about that, so I decided not to. Figuring my best option was to try anyway.

So that's how my days went for weeks and months. Falling off those bars they'd put me on, getting up again, falling down again. Needing drugs to sleep at night half the time. Spending time in the rec room they had there watching TV and staring out at a big field outside the windows.

Sometimes people would be on it playing football, having a ceremony of some kind, leading normal lives. It was good to watch 'cause sometimes it was what I wanted again, but bad too. It seemed so far away and impossible to get at through those metal framed windows. They seemed hard and cold, like the floor of that rehab room on my face every time I fell, not giving an inch between me and what I hoped for.

Then I'd think about those choppers that never came. Reliving it about every other night.

Sometimes they'd show up in my dreams, circling like that one at the bridge. Then they'd just fly away like they couldn't see us dying while Kim and those children breathed their last. The more I though about it, the angrier I got. The angrier I got, the less I tried until finally I wasn't making any progress at all. Just falling.

Sitting in that same rec room a month or so later, bruised up from another useless physical therapy session, a wheel chair rolled up next to me with a kid in it.

I was watching the field that day. Some folks were out there playing baseball and he was really gettin' into it, talkin' to the players like he was on the field, so I figured him for a player. I'd never seen any kids down here before, so he must have escaped from some other floor.

I got a real kick out of watching him go on about those boys dropping the ball or doin' a stand up run instead of slidin'. Finally I had to ask,"So what position do you play?".

He looked at me, startled a bit, then blushed a little and smiled, "Short stop sir." Well he had some manners, but I had to correct him, telling him not to call me sir 'cause I was just a Marine Sergeant.

Well that got a real reaction out of him, his head snapped around with his mouth wide open, "A marine? You're a Marine Sergeant!?"

"Well yes sir." I teased him a little.

That boy was just into the Marines. He went off then, talking about his Dad in the Navy and how he wanted to be a Marine himself, asking me every question under the sun about how I got in, where I'd been, what I'd been doing, and where I was going.

Well I wasn't so high on the Marines just then, but I didn't want to discourage him too much. So I padded it up a little and gave him a story I thought he could handle, being as honest as I could at least. I let him know it wasn't a rose garden but that didn't seem to bother him at all.

It went like that for some weeks I guess. Hearing him go on about how great I was got me going some and I really poured it on in rehab. I was on crutches inside of a month and they went on about it being a miracle. Well...I guess it was.

214

The boys name was Denny and I really looked forward to seeing him. Turned out there was a children's ward of some kind a few of floors up and he managed to escape on a pretty regular basis. That was all right with me.

We'd talk, watch the field, and I even managed to get us some western's on the television. I think it was "Hondo" and some other old serials. We'd yell at the TV and shoot at the bad guys. It really took me back. That boy just about saved my life I've got to say.

Then one day he just stopped coming down.

 I waited a few days, then did a little escaping of my own and got up to I think it was the third flour. Hobbling up and down the halls I finally found a nurse and asked about him. She knew exactly who I meant without even checking her records. She just said, "Oh…he went home."

Well it was a little disappointing, but I was glad he'd got out. I knew it was making him a little crazy being cooped up in that place. As much as I'd appreciated him being there I was glad he was finally on the other side of that window.

A week or to later I was down to one cane and starting to feel like I'd really done something. I was in that same rec room watching the field when a nurse came and said I had a lady visitor and would I see her. Well female company was ALWAYS welcome around here so of course I said yes. Some of the other boys even whistled at me a little.

She was older than me, but still pretty with a kind of careworn expression on her face like she had a story to tell. She did, she was Denny's mother.

We introduced ourselves and she explained how much my friendship had meant to Denny during his stay at Balboa. Thanking me for taking the time to be his pal since his own Dad couldn't be there. I had to thank her then, explaining he'd really helped get me motivated and what a joy he was to be around.

She smiled and nodded, then started crying. Well I didn't know what to do. I never could figure out women. I patted her on the back tentatively and asked if there was anything I could do. The next thing I knew we were hugging and I was about to cry myself.

She settled herself a little and sat down. "John...", she about whispered, "what did they tell you about Denny." I told her they said he'd gone home and I was happy for him and hoped she'd tell him so.

Pursing her lips for a moment, she said in a trembling voice, "John...he didn't go home."

Staring at her while that sank in, I took a chair asking what she meant though I already half knew. She explained that he'd had a cancer called Leukemia and he'd never really had a chance. I managed to disbelieve it anyway for a minute or two; talking about how full of life he was every time I saw him.

"Yeah," she said hoarsely," he was like that right up to the end. Full of energy."

Pausing for a moment, my lips trembling, I told her the one thing I hoped might help her. "I believe I'm walking because of that boy." Telling her the whole story then how I was about ready to give up when we met. How we both loved baseball and westerns. What a good friend he was.

She took it all in with shining eyes, anxious to hear news about her boy like any good mother. I believe I did cry a little then as she gave me another hug and said goodbye, thanking me again. I had to thank her for raising such a fine son too.

A week later, I didn't even need the canes anymore. Denny would've wanted that. A month after that I was jogging a little. Another month or so and I was marked fit for discharge to light duty.

My hands still shook some, but I could walk a straight line and feed myself. That was good enough for me and the Marines both I guess.

They assigned me to El Toro at the Quartermasters under the command of the CID. Something was going on there and they wanted me to report weekly about anything fishy. So I packed mess kits, sorted clothes, did pretty much whatever and just kept half an eye open. They had me reporting to the Doctor's at camp Pendleton weekly to make sure my wounds were healing properly and the therapy was sticking.

It was a pretty decent bunch of fellows really and we got to be friends as far as I was concerned. They got to where they'd throw me in the back of the car and haul me around with 'em when they went out. I was glad for the company too since I didn't know anybody in California except the folks I was staying with off base.

During that time the shaking got a little worse, and remembering things started getting harder. Everything except my time in Vietnam, which I still got to relive just about nightly. That didn't seem to bother these fellows though. They were honestly concerned and really helped me out every way they could, treating me better than anybody ever had in the Marines.

That made it all the more disappointing when it finally happened. I was driving around with my new buddies when they stopped the car and threw a bag over the base fence.

These were my friends, the only people I knew that'd been decent to me in the Marines from about day one, and here I was with orders to report what they'd just done. Putting it off as long as I could I did finally, reluctantly obey orders. Telling them what I'd seen, I tried to play it down as much as I could, but you can just imagine how that sweet little piece of pie went over with my superiors at the CID.

I guess that assignment was some kind of test 'cause the next thing I knew I was handed orders to report for transport back to Vietnam! Well hurrah for the Corp. They really knew how to reward loyalty, and I was about pissed off by then.

Reporting that to my doctor at Pendleton, he made short work of it, declaring me entirely unfit for combat duty and putting me on what I think they called "medical review". You got that right son! I guess I could've gone back, sat in a bunker and shook for another year trying to remember why I was there. Maybe I should've.

They had me stationed back at Pendleton then pulling light guard duty. Well I wanted to be home with my Daddy, as much as I could, since there was no telling' when he'd pass on.

I didn't much care to be there anyway so I just up and left when I didn't have any scheduled duty. I'd catch a plane back home and come back in time for my next shift like a regular job. Sometimes late, sometimes not.

I tell you what boy, they didn't like me doin' that at ALL, but there wasn't any amount of yellin' or threatening' from the Gunny, the Lieutenant, OR the Captain that made a dent on me. They couldn't really punish me the way they'd like anyway 'cause I was on medical review.

Well about the next trip, after the Captain had explained it to me I was standing in front of a full bird Colonel who knew how to dress down a non-com! He gave it to me good while I stood at full attention and said "SIR YES SIR!" whenever he asked me if I understood.

Well now I have to admit he'd scared me pretty good.

When it came right down to it though that weekend, I sat for a while thinking about my Daddy, then I thought about that Colonel. Well, there was just no way wasn't I going to spend as much time with my Daddy as I could at that point so I up and LEFT.

Next thing I knew I was standing in front of a GENERAL. He looked at the paperwork and asked me a few quiet questions. I explained about my Daddy's heart, and how pissed off I was at the Marines by now anyway. The way I had it figured the General here would either kill me or cure me so I might as well give it to him straight up.

He thought it over for a minute and just laughed. "Well son, that's a real mess." he finally confessed. "Tell you what, you just go on home and stay there while the Medical Review finishes and we'll see what happens then." Well brother that sounded just about right to me. I gave him about the last heartfelt salute I ever gave a Marine and caught the next plane outta there.

I was still a Marine, so they kept sending me my full Sergeants pay. I pretty much had to wear my marine uniforms since I didn't have civilian clothes that fit me any more.

Now I've got to say havin' that uniform on, some money to throw around, and plenty of time to treat a girl right didn't hurt my love life any. I still had Kim on my mind, but there was nothing I could do except watch her die in my dreams, so I started dating again. Not that any of them made an impression on me after being with a real woman like Kim, but I did date all three sisters in one family then started on another.

Those several months at home the only girl that got under my skin was one I really didn't date, Sue Waltrop. She'd just come over and sit around with us. Now, everybody knew what she was after, but she was just as nice and pleasant as she could be, helping out around the house and such so they got to where they just loved having her around.

Mama would talk her up 'cause she was so nice and I couldn't help but notice that. Daddy even seemed to take a shine to her. She'd even wait on me to come home after dates! Now any girl that would put up with that had some quality as far as I was concerned so I did finally ask her out.

I'd never figured she was the type for me, but we got on pretty famously I have to say. We cut a pretty good rug together and she loved hanging on my arm wherever we went and looked good doin'it! She was the first woman I'd met since Kim that really made me feel like a man, like she needed me.

I couldn't really tell her about Kim since she'd tell Mama and Daddy's health was still not too good. So I couldn't explain why I couldn't marry her, not yet anyway. We talked about it and she suggested moving in together!

Wanting desperately to be loved again, needing a woman in my life, I knew it wouldn't make my parents very happy and I wasn't so sure it was the right thing myself, but I went with it. I reckon that was as close as I knew I could get to marrying anybody else right then anyway and I needed her about as much or more than she seemed to need me. I've got to admit I'm a little ashamed of it but that's what I did.

Deciding to set up house in Salt Lake, I went and rounded us up a little apartment not too far from downtown so we could walk where we needed. I told her all about the place and she got genuinely excited! The next day I got a few pieces of furniture, a lamp and a couple of end tables, and went to deliver them.

I can't explain what happened then. I just drove around and around and could NOT for the LIFE of me remember where that apartment was! It was like I'd just lost my mind. I knew I'd had a little trouble remembering things before but nothing like THIS! Oh my goodness, there was no WAY on God's green earth I could face Sue after that. I didn't know what to do. Going home I just sat on the couch and watched television, switching channels until Daddy begged for mercy. Sue would call but I'd just tell them I didn't want to talk to her and they'd make some excuse. Thankfully she was too busy to come over for the next couple of days.

Next thing I knew Mama said the Marines were on the phone. It was my Doctor at Pendleton requesting I go back to California for a final examination. Well I wasn't sure I liked how final their final examination sounded, but I was glad for ANY excuse to get out of Utah just then and just flat WENT.

Well that doctor looked me up and down and asked about symptoms. I explained about forgetting the apartment and told him I still hurt some. He pushed my ribs a little, rotated my leg joints until I yelled uncle, looked in every orifice available with a wide variety of flashlights, then sat at his desk looking thoughtful for a minute while he peeled off a rubber glove.

"Well son," he interrupted his own revelry after a thoughtful silence, "It's still hard to tell, but I've been given permission to do whatever I see fit here." Fixing me with a stare for a full minute, he asked finally "So do you still want to be a Marine?" Well I'd seen enough Marine Corp to last me a lifetime so it didn't take me long to formulate a respectful "No sir."

He took a big rubber stamp out of a drawer, rolled it dramatically back and forth across an ink pad and slammed it down on the paperwork on his desk. "Well son, I guess you get your wish." he finished, handing the papers to me.

So just like that I wasn't a Marine any more. I'd been in so long I wasn't sure what to do with myself for a while. Turn's out California is full of people like that so I figured I'd give it a try! I'd been living off base in a rented room with a Sheriffs deputy named Ed Vanderburgh and his family while I was stationed at Pendleton before, so I just went back and picked up where I'd left off!

They liked me just fine so I set about trying to find my niche in California. I went for my first job interview, I was so excited, the lady went over my application, and said, I see you served in Vietnam, I said yes, and she said, we don't hire baby killers here. I just about hit the floor, I did an about face, and got out of that place. I bussed some tables, did some construction work, even sang backup in a band for a while, but nothing seemed to fit. Something would always happen that'd mess it up for me. I'd shake too much for one job, not remember enough for another, or just generally piss off somebody I shouldn't 'cause of my hard earned disrespect for authority from the Marines.

Well I thanked Ed and his family for putting up with me, told them I'd be in touch, and left back to Utah.

I tell you what boy, I looked all over the place for a job with Daddy driving me to every interview. It didn't take long for me to get tired of being told I didn't have enough of whatever it took to get just about any job short of flipping hamburgers. Even THOSE fellows wouldn't talk to me after they saw my hands shaking. I just didn't have the education, job skills background, or ANYTHING to qualify for even basic jobs and nobody wanted me, no way, no how for no kind of work under the sun!

During that time I actually did meet up with Sue again. I'm not sure what kind of line my parents had given her but we rekindled our little romance. We never really discussed my leaving her before and I was glad for it 'cause I STILL didn't know what'd happened there. I have to say she was about as understanding as a woman can get and I was about ready to ask her to move in with ME by that time. I was ready for ANTYHING to get something good in my life and she was lookin' like it to me son.

Daddy did finally and actually die then. He had another heart attack and went in to the doctor, but he'd fooled us so many times we all would just about laugh with him about it.

Then the doctors started talking to him about open heart surgery and son we got SERIOUS. This was the seventies and that was the real deal, neck or nothing, final option back then and the survival rate was less than I'd allow for.

 They talked him into believing that was the miracle cure for all his troubles though. Well I guess it might have been if he hadn't contracted hepatitis during the operation. I always thought they were just sugar coating his best option anyway.

Mama didn't want me to go see him at first when she found out what he had. She'd fought too hard for too long to keep us both in her life and just plain wouldn't let me, afraid to lose us both. She did finally relent after some discussion from the doctors.

So I took the night watch.

Finally, getting some time alone with my Daddy was as wonderful now as it had always been. I sat with him quietly for a few days. It took me back to my time in Vietnam. Death seemed about like an old friend by now and I'd sometimes stand silently beside Daddy's bed, warding off some unseen presence.

Then I started talking to him.

Just little things at first. How I'd stood watch in Okinawa and the Airbase…and Song. Seemed to me like he could hear me then for some reason, like he wanted to hear more. We'd never really talked about it since I got back.

The thought of my Daddy leaving this world without knowing who his own son was just seemed wrong to me then and I poured out my heart to him. Told him everything that'd happened while I was gone. Everything that I'd left behind. All the dreams that were crushed. All the people I'd met. The crazy things that happened.

Finally, at last, I told him about Kim. I laughed and cried, knowing somehow this was getting through to him, helping him somehow. I knew it so strong that when he did finally slip away in the night, I figured the only reason he'd held on so long was to hear what had happened next.

Dying is something you only do once, so I guess it was fine with me that Daddy took his own sweet time getting it done. Just like my Daddy to make sure we were ready to go. Ready to go home. Ready to go to Utah. Ready to go out into the world.

Ready for him to die.

We buried him in Kaysville, Utah, with full Military honors. I expect I'll be joining him there soon with the same guns firing over my grave. Maybe I even deserve it.

Sue was there with me at the funeral. She'd been with me the whole time I wasn't with Daddy, giving me her support. I honestly wished I could marry her, but I just couldn't bring myself to ask when I saw Kim in my dreams every other night.

Some friends of mine, Ned Chambers and his girlfriend came by with Sue a week or two after dad's funeral with some exciting news. They'd decided to get married and wanted me and Sue to be their witnesses in Reno!

Well, a little trip sounded pretty good to me so I agreed and off we went that weekend! Watching the desert roll by took my mind off life and Sue was just a ray of sunshine the whole time. We held hands and listened to Ned and his fiancée make plans.

Rolling into Reno we decided to get them hitched up then and have some fun afterwards. Getting the license squared away we got the justice of the peace lined up. Sue picked out some flowers for the bride to be and I held Ned by the arm to make sure he didn't get away since he was my ride and all. Not that he needed much persuading; she was a real looker I've got to say!

Lining up in front of that JP, they started begging us to join them! Well I confess I was a little confused at first, it wasn't like joining the YMCA, and it was MARRIAGE for cryin' out loud! Did they just think I would up and...well, looking over at Sue she was about as beautiful and a little embarrassed.

Still, excusing myself for lack of money, I had to confess to poverty sufficient to rob the good justice of his hard earned fee. Well he was apparently in a good enough mood and my friends good enough persuasion, that he declared a two for one special right then and there!

Good lord.

Well what could I say to that? Sue was standing there as beautiful as I'd ever seen her, and everybody was so excited. Now Sue was as understanding and forgiving a woman as I'd ever met, but I just didn't see HOW she'd forgive me if I walked away from her now. I tell you what boy, it was now or never so I jumped in with BOTH feet!

The JP got on with his "do you take so and so's" and we gave all the right answers. I remember him declaring us all men and wives by the power and authority granted him by the state of Nevada and just like that boy we were MARRIED!

That was about as happy as I'd been in a solid year. But it turned out Sue wanted a MARINE with some MONEY! She wasn't settling for an ex-marine with a failing savings account and no job prospects.

We argued and fought like nobodies business and I guess I saw what she really was then. She'd done her part being nice and if I wasn't gonna do mine settin' her up then she wasn't stickin' around. Turned out she'd prefer a truck driver with a steady income over me and the next one that came along had her in the front seat.

I guess it was love though. Last I heard he'd quit his job and she'd been supporting him by clerking at a convenience store for fifteen years. Love stinks I guess.

Heart broken, body broken, still dreaming about Kim, still unable to get a job, I was just sick. I needed to go back where the blacktop ended, desperately needed to get back some piece of where I'd been. So I decided to try one more time. My sister Irene said I might find a job in Mobile, So I went.

Three months later, turned down for job after job because of my medical disability, I was right back where I started all right. My Uncles had said they'd find me a job, but one after the other had to confess they couldn't help me. Oh they tried I know, but I was just too strange, too changed from what I'd been, too unable to be what they expected.

Unemployed in Southern Alabama, I boarded another bus right back to Utah.

It felt like drowning all over again and I put out every feeler I could, applied for everything I could think of and some stuff I couldn't. No, no, no, no, NO!! Some stamped it, some said it, some just said "we'll call you" but it all meant the same thing. I'd failed AGAIN!

I wasn't ready to die yet though so I stuck my hand out of the water one last time, applying for a bunch of federal position I knew for a FACT I wasn't qualified for. Daddy must have been watching over me then, cause I just about felt his strong hand grab me by the wrist.

Out of the blue, I got a call from the Treasury Department! The Director there said he could use a young man with my background (meaning military). It was called the "Upward Mobility" program. I'd have to finish High School, and go on to College but they'd let me attend school half the day, work half they day, and still pay me full time!

Good God almighty! It was about all I could do to stop saying "THANK YOU LORD!" in my mind long enough to ask him to let me sleep on it. He VERY graciously gave me the time.

Thinkin' about my life as I faded to sleep that night, I honestly wasn't sure I was ready to fail at something as big as this.

Drifting through my childhood I saw Shorty and Roy, Grandpa, Daddy, Kim, and even Cory. I was in boot camp again with Easy screaming in my face. Wandering through Vietnam a while, I saw all the things I usually did about every night when I closed my eyes.

All the death I'd seen, all the love I'd lost, all my failures since I'd returned from over there formed a mocking parade for me with Sue at the very end screaming the last words she'd said to me as she walked out. "You'll NEVER amount to ANYTHING Bob Mizell!"

The door slammed shut on that tiny apartment and I shot out of bed, tangled in sweat soaked sheets. So I did the only thing that made any sense to me.

I called that man back and became an ACCOUNTANT!

Well…things got better then. We'll have to talk about it sometime.

Please remember that, WHERE THE BLACKTOP ENDS, is Biographical Fiction, that said, the old home place in Mobile, Alabama , is surrounded, by houses, and businesses, now, I've heard that they built a water bottling plant, right over , where the old outhouses were. Every time , I have bottled water, I have to look, to see where it was made.

Late on these long cold, Utah nights, when I'm in a deep sleep, I can still hear, Kim calling me.

John lives with his wife Mary, and seven wonderful grand children in Sunset, Utah, enjoying his retirement.

semper fi

Made in the USA
Columbia, SC
23 April 2018